AN ANVIL ORIGINAL

*Under the general editorship of Louis L. Snyder*

# THE AGE OF
# THE REFORMATION

## ROLAND H. BAINTON †

*Titus Street Professor Emeritus
of Ecclesiastical History
Yale University*

KRIEGER PUBLISHING COMPANY
MALABAR, FLORIDA

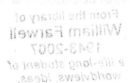

Original Edition 1956
Reprint Edition 1984

Printed and Published by
**ROBERT E. KRIEGER PUBLISHING COMPANY, INC.**
**KRIEGER DRIVE**
**MALABAR, FLORIDA 32950**

## Library of Congress Cataloging in Publication Data

Bainton, Roland Herbert, 1894 -
   The age of the Reformation.

   "An Anvil original."
   Reprint. Originally published: Princeton, N.J.: Van Nostrand, 1956.
   Bibliography: p.
   Includes index.
   1. Reformation.   2. Reformation—Sources.   I. Title.
BR305.2.B295   1984                    270.6                    83-25145
ISBN 0-89874-736-8

10      9      8      7      6

Dedicated to my graduate students who have written their doctoral dissertations in the field of Reformation studies. They are now serving in the institutions indicated:

## On Luther

Nils Arne Bendts, Theological Seminary, Sumatra, Indonesia

Robert H. Fischer, Lutheran Theological Seminary, Mayfield, Illinois

Warren C. Hovland, Oregon State College, Corvallis, Oregon

John R. Von Rohr, Pacific School of Religion, Berkeley, California

## On Calvin

Henry Barnard Kuizenga, Pastor, Ann Arbor, Michigan

John H. Leith, Pastor, Presbyterian Church, Auburn, Alabama

William M. Thompson, Union Theological Seminary, Richmond, Virginia (deceased)

## On Melanchthon

Clyde L. Manschreck, Duke University, Durham, North Carolina

## On the Hungarian Reformation

William Toth, Franklin Marshall, Lancaster, Pennsylvania

## On the Anglican Reformation

John M. Krumm, Chaplain, Columbia University, New York

## On the Anabaptists, Refugees and Advocates of Liberty

John W. Brush, Andover-Newton Theological Seminary, North Newton, Massachusetts

Franklin H. Littell, Bad Godesberg, Germany

Frederick A. Norwood, Garrett Biblical Institute, Evanston, Illinois

Paul Schwab, Trinity University, San Antonio, Texas

Frank Wray, Beria College, Beria, Kentucky

Lowell H. Zuck, Eden Theological Seminary, Webster Groves, Missouri

# PREFACE

The Age of the Reformation was an age of upheaval. With regard to every such era dispute arises as to whether events precipitated ideas or ideas incited events. Undoubtedly travel, discovery, invention, and the consolidation of power prompted reflection about institutions and about the ultimate problems of life. Yet throughout the history of the West, where the Reformation took place, ideas have fashioned events. The emergence of Christendom is inconceivable apart from the Christian faith. The disintegration of Christendom could easily have come without a resurgence of faith. What did happen in the sixteenth century was really not a disintegration. To this day we talk about the culture of the West. And this is just an attenuated terminology for what was once called Christendom. The religious revolution of the sixteenth century shattered an ecclesiastical structure and quickened a universal faith. Despite all the division, the ability of Western man still to talk in terms of a universal justice, humanity, and the rights of man is derived from a Christian heritage which the Reformation revitalized and transmitted to our time.

As to the telling of the story, there are two methods which the Anvil books combine, a combination which is employed in this book. The first method is to reconstruct what one takes to have happened on the basis of the collection, evaluation, and interpretation of sources. The second is to let the sources speak for themselves. The assumption that they can is fatuous. Of course, given enough sources, they do, but even so not without subjection to critical scrutiny. The literature of reform commonly exaggerates the evils to be corrected. The historian has to be on the sharp lookout for any unwitting concessions or conceded facts with contrary implications. Source must be set against source. The selection of sources introduces subjective judgments as to importance. Objectivity is an ideal, which may be approximated but never fully achieved.

The difficulty in this book is greater than in others of the series because documents have been abridged. By this device a much larger range can be covered and a more balanced picture achieved. Still, opinions may well differ as to whether the excerpting has been sound and fair. The concerned reader will always do well to go on from such excerpts as these to documents unabridged.

*New Haven, Connecticut*            ROLAND H. BAINTON

# ACKNOWLEDGMENTS

Thanks are due to the publishers who have kindly granted permission to the author to reproduce the following from their publications.

Reading No. 1, IV: From R. H. Bainton, *Here I Stand* (Abingdon-Cokesbury, 1950)

Reading No. 3, II: *Ibid.*

Reading No. 5, VII: From H. C. Vedder, *Balthasar Hubmaier* (G. P. Putnam's Sons, 1905)

Reading No. 7, I-II, IV-VI: From H. Gee and W. J. Hardy, *Documents Illustrative of English Church History* (St. Martin's Press, 1914); III, from *First and Second Prayer-Books of Edward the Sixth* (Everyman's Library, E. P. Dutton & Co., Inc., 1910)

Reading No. 10, I: From R. H. Bainton, *Here I Stand* (Abingdon-Cokesbury, 1950)

Reading No. 11, II: From W. S. Hudson, *John Ponet, Advocate of Limited Monarchy* (Copyright 1942, by the University of Chicago Press); V, with permission of G. Bell & Sons, Ltd.

Hymn quoted on p. 83 from *The Hymnal*, courtesy of Presbyterian Board of Christian Education

# TABLE OF CONTENTS

6

# Part I

# THE AGE OF THE REFORMATION

# — 1 —

# INTRODUCTION

**The Sixteenth Century.** The sixteenth century was the Age of the Reformation. It was, of course, the age of much else besides. It might also be called the Age of Discovery, for in the wake of the *Santa Maria* there came the navigators and the conquistadores. Nevertheless, in the sixteenth century the New World had not as yet made a decisive impact upon the Old. The effect may have been greatest in the economic sphere through the influx of bullion from the Spanish possessions, but not until the seventeenth century did the Americas, to any large degree, offer an asylum to the oppressed, an area for social and political experimentation to the hardy, and an opportunity for improvement to the disinherited of Europe.

The sixteenth century was also an age of science and more so than the preceding one hundred years. In fact, if one can talk of the Renaissance in science, it must be placed a century after the great flowering of art and letters in Italy of the fifteenth and early sixteenth centuries. Curiously, the year which in Church history may be taken to demarcate the Renaissance from the Counter-reformation, the year 1542 which saw the establishment of the Roman Inquisition (*see Reading 8, No. III*) was the very year of the publication of the *Anatomy* of Vesalius and the year following, 1543, saw the appearance of the work of Copernicus, *On the Revolution of the Heavenly Spheres*. Yet, despite these and other great discoveries, the sixteenth century cannot properly be called the age of science. The full impact of the new findings

11

was not to be felt until later, for in the 1500's men did not look to natural science to solve the problems and answer the riddles of life, nor was there as yet a great crisis in Christendom over the conflict of science and religion. As late as the eighteenth century, theologians as well as scientists believed that the astronomers in particular were but thinking God's thoughts after Him. Only in the nineteenth century did geology and biology relegate Genesis to religious mythology.

The sixteenth century was an age of faith. It was even more an age of faith than the preceding period. For a parallel, one must go back several hundred years to the days of the First Crusade or even to the founding of the Inquisition. In the period of the Reformation men were ready both to die and to kill for religion, to divide families and to disrupt kingdoms rather than renounce the truth of God. The Reformation actually arrested an incipient secularism and made religion and even confessionalism dominant concerns even in politics for another 150 years.

The Reformation was both Protestant and Catholic. The two parties to this day are not at one in their interpretation of the events. The Protestants call the Catholic Reformation the Counter-reformation. To a degree it was, because manifestly it opposed the Protestant Reformation and incontestably was stimulated by it, but did not originate out of opposition, for a Catholic reformation was underway before the emergence of Luther and at the peak was not wholly consumed in counter measures. One of the great endeavors of the Catholic Reformation was the evangelization of the New World. The Catholics, in turn, sometimes call their movement The Reformation and the Protestant the Pseudo-reformation. Obviously, the historian of this period is not poking ashes without embers, and he does well at the outset to avow his own affiliation. The writer of this book is a staunch Protestant. At the same time he kneels before the shrine of historical objectivity. Let it be hoped that the two are not mutually exclusive.

**Causes of the Reformation.**   There are three schools of interpretation with regard to the origins of the Reformation, particularly in its Protestant form. The first is moral, the second doctrinal, and the third sociological.

The first maintains the basic cause of the Reformation in all its forms to have been the undeniable moral corruption of the Church. Some Catholic historians have contended that the Protestant Reformation was a continuation of the abuses through the abrogation of the rules. Clerical concubinage, for example, was ended not by clerical celibacy but by clerical marriage. Other Catholic historians have said that the early Protestants were passionate moral reformers whose inordinate zeal carried them beyond the bounds of obedience.

Another school maintains that the correction of moral corruption was only an incidental concern of Luther and his associates. The attack was rather against the teaching of the Church. In general this has been a Protestant interpretation, though recently some Catholic historians concur. The Catholic Reformation, of course, also involved doctrine. The third school looks more to changes in the structure of society, urbanization, commercialism and nationalism, adjustment to which on the part of the Church occasioned convulsions of diverse sorts.

As to the first approach: moral abuses unquestionably concerned all of the reformers, whether Catholic or Protestant. The difference was as to precisely what should be considered an abuse and what should be the remedy. At this point a memorandum compiled by the Cardinals and submitted to Pope Paul III in 1538 on *The Reform of the Church* (*see Reading 8, No. I*) may be instructively compared with Luther's arraignment in his *Address to the Christian Nobility of the German Nation* (*see Reading 2, No. V*).

The Cardinals centered on abuses parochial, financial, judicial, and moral. As to the parochial: the cure of souls, complained the Cardinals, was neglected because unworthy and uninstructed candidates were ordained to the ministry. Foreigners were given sees they could not serve, and many of the clergy were constantly nonresident. On the financial side objection was registered against pluralities, i.e., the conferring on one person of several income-yielding benefices; also against expectations whereby for a fee an expectancy was granted to a see not yet vacant, and likewise against commutations whereby a vow was remitted in favor of a financial contribution. General reference was made to simony which is strictly the buying of any ecclesiastical office. The dispensing of indulgences should be, said the Cardinals, restricted to once a year in a single locality. In the judicial sphere complaint was made of dispensations whereby again for a fee exemption was granted from the laws of the Church. The great moral abuse was the position of honor accorded prostitutes in Rome. Doctrinal abuses were held not to exist because the teaching of the Church is inerrant. The only concern was that the truth should not be corrupted by the teaching of sceptical professors, nor suborned by the unedifying *Colloquies* of Erasmus.

Luther was more caustic and devastating partly because he was voicing the century-old complaints of the Germans against the exploitation of their land by Italian Popes. His indictment of the pomp, luxury, and extravagance of the heads of the Church, including the Cardinals, was naturally more trenchant than the complaints emanating from the Sacred College, though there was much agreement, notably with regard to the neglect of the cure of souls and as to the judicial abuses. Luther went further in his demand for the restriction of appeals; on the matter of sexual immorality the Cardinals referred only to the prostitutes at Rome and made no mention of the system of clerical concubinage, tolerated and taxed, which Luther excoriated. The difference is most significant at the point of the remedy. The Cardinals would enforce the rule of celibacy for the clergy. Luther would abolish the rule and allow clerical marriage.

Yet, for Luther this was not the primary ground of objection. He said himself that what differentiated him from previous reformers was that, whereas they attacked the life, he attacked the doctrine. By so doing he compelled the Catholics to reexamine and more tightly formulate their own position. The Catholic answer was to displace the prevalent scholastic theology by another of an earlier vintage. Occamism, then popularly called Modernism, was displaced by Thomism. A word with regard to these two systems. The Thomistic position is that all truth can be rationally integrated by a system of ascending levels. The natural man by his reason and conscience can attain to the knowledge of the God and can apprehend that universal morality called natural law. The higher reaches of theology, including God's trinitarian structure, are attainable only by revelation, just as the loftier Christian virtues require the assistance of special divine grace, but nature leads up to grace and reason to revelation which, once given, can be explicated by reason. The entire structure of theology, the Church, and society is further integrated by the assumption that reality consists of universals, i.e., entities which embrace and relate particular manifestations. The Church and the State and even the Trinity are not aggregates of unrelated individuals but are gathered rather in a nexus of corporate being.

This theology was challenged by Occamism. It denied the universals, claiming rather that reality consists of particular single individuals related only by contiguity in space and time. Consequently the State is not a universal corporate entity but only the sum of its citizens; likewise the Church of its members. On this assumption the State tends to be based on contract between members, and the Church on covenant. When this view is applied to the Trinity, if the three persons are individuals related only by contiguity in space and time, then they become three gods. Such was the answer of philosophy, but since the Church had ruled that they are not three gods, theology and philosophy must diverge. The result is the doctrine of double truth or at least of double logic. The teaching of the Church no longer supported by reason was compelled therefore to fall back on arbitrary authority. This Modernism the Catholic Reformation rejected and reverted to Thomism.

Some Catholic interpreters agree that the Protestant Reformation was doctrinal in the sense that it was derived from scholastic Modernism. Basically this is not so. The individualism of Luther was of another sort, as we shall see. He had been trained as a Modernist, to be sure, but he was not interested, at bottom, in philosophy at all. Greater weight may be given to the claim that he was influenced by this movement to locate authority in the Bible. Even here, however, what else could he have done, when he rejected the authority of the Church, other than to appeal to the authority of the Scriptures?

Yet Luther's Reformation was doctrinal because it was

profoundly religious. Not so much the ideas of Modernism repelled him as the temperature. His development
will be more fully delineated in the next section, but
the difference can well be illustrated now by taking the
case of indulgences. They were introduced at the time
of the Crusades. First, those who took the cross were
accorded whatever merits would have accrued had they
stayed at home and engaged in some pious exercise such
as a pilgrimage. Next, indulgences were granted to those
who, unable to go on a Crusade, made a money contribution. Such persons in return might receive a remission
of penalties imposed upon them by the Church. The
device proved so lucrative that it was extended to every
worthy object such as the building of cathedrals, hospitals, and even bridges. The noblest monuments of the
Middle Ages were financed in this way. In the meantime, claims for indulgences were staggered. They were
made to apply not only to penalties on earth but also
in purgatory. Persons already in purgatory might be
granted immediate release. Some indulgences remitted
not only penalties but also forgave sins. The theory on
which the entire practice rested was that the Pope held
the key to the treasury of the merits of the saints, who
having been better than they needed to be for their own
salvation, had acquired a store of superfluous credits and
these were regarded as transferable to others. Plainly the
practice ministered to venality. This the Cardinals,
addressing Pope Paul III, would curb by allowing but
one vending of indulgences a year in the same locality,
but Luther's objection was vastly more drastic. He denied
the treasury of the accumulated, superfluous merits of
the saints. After all of the financial abuses were corrected, he still regarded the entire transaction as an
abomination. What he demanded was not reform but
abolition. Not merely the practice but also the teaching
was at fault, and not simply was it false but an abomination in the eyes of God.

   **The Sociological Background.**   The third school of
modern historians would interpret the Reformation less
in moral and doctrinal than in sociological terms. A
recent author has outlined the changes in the structure
of society and the accommodations of the Catholic
Church during the period of the Renaissance. There was

taking place, he suggests, "a transition from a civilization predominantly feudal and ecclesiastical in its social,
political and cultural manifestations and agrarian in its
foundations, to another predominantly national, urban,
secular and laic, in which the economic center of
gravity had shifted from agriculture to commerce and
industry and in which a simple money economy had
evolved into capitalism." [1]

The attempt of the Church to adjust to the new urban
economy based on coin rather than on kind gave rise to
some of the financial abuses already enumerated, and
conflicts with the national states over money entailed
political changes. The immediate produce of the land
had been the basis of the Church's financial structure
in the early Middle Ages. The Church could scarcely
have operated otherwise in a landed society, but the
consequence was entanglement in the feudal system with
the danger of dependence on lay lords. The new economy
offered a way to obviate this by drawing revenues not
directly from lands often in lay hands but through levies
on the local churches to be paid in coin. To this, however, the rising national monarchies objected, and in the
first instance France. The papacy, depleted of resources,
succumbed to France, and the residence of the Popes
was transferred to Avignon for a period called the Babylonian Captivity because it was roughly seventy years in
duration (1309-1377).

During that period the attempt continued unabated to
centralize the wealth of the Church by levies on the local
sees. Pope John XXII, in particular, exploited and devised
such expedients as annates, reservations, expectations,
commutations and others, and the French crown objected
little, inasmuch as the money was not to cross the Alps.
The subjection of the papacy to France, however, occasioned such disaffection in other lands that the secession
manifest in the Protestant Reformation was in danger of
anticipation by some 200 years. To avert this the Pope
returned to Rome. The Cardinals, however, remained in
France and elected another Pope. There followed the

[1] Wallace K. Ferguson, "The Church in a Changing World, a
Contribution to the Interpretation of the Renaissance,"
*The American Historical Review,* Vol. 59, No. 1, October,
1953, pp. 1-18.

Papal Schism lasting until 1417. Attempts were made to end the scandal by the summoning of councils, and they in turn undertook the reform of the Church, but every effort proved abortive. Conciliarism was impotent because the conflict with the rising, consolidated, national monarchies required an increasingly centralized government on the side of the Church. In the end the papacy overcame conciliarism, but only at the price of recognizing the sovereignty of the national states. Conceding this, the Popes then made separate bargains called concordats with the nations.

All of this involved a great recession from the universal claim and the universal jurisdiction which the Church had once exercised at the peak of the feudal period. By way of compensation the Church in the Renaissance entrenched itself in Italy. The papacy became one of the Italian powers, and the Popes behaved like the despots of the city-states, cunning in diplomacy, ruthless in war, magnificent in the arts and literature, unscrupulous and unbridled in morals. The reform movements were set over against a thoroughgoing secularization of the papacy itself. The Pope who dealt with Martin Luther, Leo X, was an elegant dilettante, a patron of artists, a gambler, hunter, and composer of elegant, impromptu Latin orations, a man who, according to a modern Catholic historian, would not have been deemed fit to be a doorkeeper in the house of the Lord had he lived in the days of the apostles.

In the social changes outlined above, some would see the basic ground of the Reformation, involving on the Catholic side a grudging relinquishment of medieval claims, a recognition of nationalism, and even a nationalizing of the Church, which in France and Spain fell under the control of the crown.

Protestantism took on the complexion of the land in which it chanced to be. With complete opportunism alliances were made with whatever power offered protection to the Word of God. This might mean Tudor absolutism, German particularism, Polish feudalism, or even extra-Europeanism under the suzerainty of the infidel Turks. The Protestants were politically conservative and only slowly and reluctantly resisted the political regimes of their particular countries. As for the control of the Church over the civil structure of society Luther renounced all this, but Calvin struck out in the direction of a new type of theocracy.

The foregoing picture of the changes taking place in the society cannot be gainsaid and, unquestionably, the Church did have to come to terms with urbanization, commercialization, nationalism, and the emergence of a lay and secular culture, but the Reformation, whether Catholic or Protestant, is not to be equated with the accommodation which, in many instances, was grudging and, when cordial, was transforming. Consider the case of lay culture, which the Catholic Reformation naturally did not foster. Instead it enhanced sacerdotalism. Protestantism did contribute to laicism but not to secularism. The priesthood of all believers was designed not to make all priests into laymen, but all laymen into priests. The net result, of course, was to demote the clerical caste, but not to diminsh the religious orientation. The Protestants desired that every member of the congregation should be as spiritual and, in so far as might be possible, as instructed in matters religious as the ministers. The Jesuits undertook the education of the Catholic masses that the laity might be religiously literate.

More attention will be given in this book to the Protestant than to the Catholic Reformation. The reason is that the Protestant movement did more to change the face of Europe. The Catholic Reformation was endeavoring to correct defections from its own ideal and to restore a waning control. The Protestants sought to alter the pattern. The hope was that all Christendom would embrace the new. The result was a shattered ecclesiastical structure. The relations of Church and State were profoundly affected. In the process of adjustment arose wars of religion—wars, at any rate, in which religion was a major component. Out of all the welter emerged new attitudes to life and to religion.

**Anticipations of the Reformation.**  The Protestant Reformation was not without its antecedents, not even at the point of the disruption of Christendom. One must not forget that the Roman Church had long since been separate from the Greek and the Russian, not to mention the smaller Eastern dissidents. The Reformation affected only the West, and even in the West the Protestant secession was but the culmination of a long series of schisms during the preceding 300 years. Curiously, the peak of the Church's theocratic control was also the period of incipient disintegration. In the age of Innocent III, when the Pope exercised a control, albeit indirect, exceeding that of any king even in matters political, at that very moment Christendom was challenged at the center by the infiltration of the Catharan heresy into southern France. In the same region and in northern Italy flourished the Waldenses. The sectarian swarm anticipated the pattern of later Protestantism at its most divisive moments. Northern Italy was in particular infested by the Patarini, Petrobrusiani, Arnoldisti, Tisserands, Humiliati and Fraticelli. In England the Lollards presaged an ecclesiastical revolution and in Bohemia the Hussites achieved one. Of all these groups only the Waldenses survived by retreat into the recesses of the Alps and the Hussites by force of arms in Bohemia. The Protestant Reformation does not stem directly from any of these sects. Yet the virulent critique which the sectaries had long hurled at the established Church cannot wholly be discounted as preparing the public mind.

Many of the ideas of the medieval sects fed at least indirectly into Protestantism in its various phases. One was moralism. Some of the earlier reformers contended that the very sacraments of the Church are invalid if administered by the unworthy. The Catholic Church holds, on the contrary, that the efficacy is of God and the unworthiness of the human ministrant in no way detracts. Yet the reformatory Pope, Gregory VII, had played into the hands of the insurgents by calling upon the laity to refuse to receive the sacraments at the hands of the married clergy. He did not say that the sacraments would do no good, only that they should be rejected in order to rebuke the ministrant. The inference, however, was not far off that misdeeds would invalidate the act.

Another subversive idea was predestination, the doctrine that some have been elected by God from before the very foundation of the world and that they are the true Church. This idea is not disruptive if there is absolutely no way of telling who are the elect, but if a worthy life be an indication of election and if an unworthy life be a fairly certain sign of reprobation, if, in other words, predestination be combined with moralism, then the deduction is obvious that a scandalous Pope does not even belong to the true Church at all. Such was the conclusion of John Wyclif.

Predestination undercut the Church from one direction. Eschatology, the doctrine of last things, assailed the Church from another. The latter was the belief in the speedy return of the Lord Jesus. Catholicism, from the days of St. Augustine, had projected the second coming of Christ indefinitely into the future and had centered attention upon the confrontation of the individual soul with its judge at the Last Day. The new eschatology weakened the authority of the great medieval theocracy by the announcement that its term was short and, if unreformed, its doom was sure. Such ideas are found among the Spiritual Franciscans and the Hussites.

Many of the sectaries attacked the theory of the sacraments, particularly of the Mass. The Fourth Lateran Council in the age of Innocent III had formulated the doctrine of transubstantiation, according to which, when the priest pronounces the words *Hoc est corpus meum,* "this is my body," the bread and the wine on the altar continue to look, taste, and feel as before. Their accidents remain the same, but their substance changes into the substance of the flesh and blood of Christ. The priest offers again this flesh and blood as a sacrifice to God, and Calvary is thus repeated. Only the priest can perform this miracle because only he is qualified through the sacrament of ordination. Inasmuch as salvation is mediated through the sacraments the priest therefore occupies a unique position. Since he is able to do for men more even than their earthly parents, who generate them only to temporal life, whereas he begets them to the eternal, his power exceeds that of any monarch who rules only over the body and not over the soul. And by virtue of this spiritual prerogative the priest acquires a right to direct, in many respects, the lives of men. To deny, then, that the Sacrament of the Mass actually brings Christ physically to the altar, to deny that the sacrifice of Calvary is repeated, to deny that the priest alone can do whatever is done, any and all of these denials demote the Church in things spiritual and temporal. Transubstantiation was denied by the Cathari, the Wyclifites and the Waldenses, and the lay element was stressed by all.

The authority of the Church was challenged from more than one angle. The Franciscans, dedicated to absolute poverty, lodged a charge of heresy against that money-raising Pope, John XXII, because of his declaration that Christ had property. The Modernists in philosophy sorely needed authority to undergird theology, but where was authority to be discovered? It could not reside in the great entities called universals of which the Church itself was one but only in individuals. But could the Pope as an individual be regarded as infallible? A negative answer was given by William of Occam who was at once the founder of the Modernists and also a Franciscan. He lived in the days of Pope John XXII and compiled a massive compendium of his errors. Occam concluded that since the gates of hell cannot prevail against the Church, someone always in the Church will be right, but there is no infallible way of knowing who it may be. The only recourse is to rely upon the authority of the Bible.

The Bible, however, was subjected to historical criticism by the Humanists, the scholars of the Renaissance. They began investigating the manuscripts and revising the texts. The greatest among them was Erasmus of Rotterdam who in his edition of the Greek New Testament in 1516—the very first printing of the New Testament in Greek—left out the famous text in First John 5: "There are three that witness in Heaven, the Father, the Spirit, and the Son," which he was unable to find in any manuscript. He promised when challenged to insert it in subsequent editions if a single manuscript could be found in which it occurred. His condition was met from a very late copy and he fulfilled his word in the third edition of 1521. Still he was unconvinced and the Church had eventually to recognize he had been right at the outset. But this meant that not the Pope but an historical expert must determine the text of the Scripture and how then could the Pope be an infallible interpreter if he were not in a position to determine the true text? In this period, of course, the Pope had not been infallibly declared to be infallible. The assumption was, however, already common.

Again there were those among the Humanists and the Mystics such as the Brethren of the Common Life and the

Friends of God who centered piety on the love of God and the service of the neighbor in the imitation of the lowly Jesus. They decried theological speculation. Such a position was not in conflict with the teachings of the Church, only indifferent to certain aspects. Yet such a view meant that Thomism would have to be regarded as inconsequential and the emphasis upon the imitation of Christ was a standing rebuke to churchmen who behaved more like the rulers of the Gentiles. The sectaries such as Wyclif and Hus were particularly fond of drawing a disparaging contrast between Christ refusing a crown and the Pope wearing a three-tiered tiara, more imposing than the single-layered crown of an emperor.

— 2 —

# THE OUTBREAK OF THE LUTHERAN REVOLT

The Lutheran revolt does not stem directly from the medieval sects. Quite enough was amiss to provoke a rebellion, as it were, without ancestry. When, however, Luther got under way, many were attracted to him by reason of the earlier moulding of the public mind through the sectarian movements, and he himself came gradually, to his own amazement, to endorse some of the ideas of those in former times burned at the stake, such as John Hus.

Luther was a German. That of itself is something. The Germans had long been complaining of the exactions of the papacy, which were more felt in Germany because the land was retarded as to national consolidation, and no strong government was in a position to repulse papal encroachments. Not infrequently Luther excoriated the avarice and arrogance of the Italian Curia. Some historians feel that the Protestant Reformation was basically a revolt of the Teutonic peoples against a Latin culture. Here is another sociological interpretation. A certain plausibility is given to this thesis in view of the eventual configuration, with Protestantism established north of the Rhine and Catholicism to the south. But this generalization is not to be overdone. There were sizable minorities in all countries. In France, at one time, the majority of the upper classes was Protestant. Italy had a respectable faction, though Spain admittedly had but very few. Germany never did become entirely Protestant. Bavaria in the sixteenth century, as it is largely now, was prevailingly Catholic. The great strength of the Protestants was and is in the area which is now the East Zone of Germany. England has always had some Catholic recusants, and the Scandinavian countries would have had more had it not been for pressure from the State.

This operated in all countries and drew the lines much more sharply than unconstrained persuasion of the populace would have done. All rulers, Protestants included, inherited from the Christian Roman Empire the view that a state cannot thrive without the support of religion. Only one religion can be true and that religion should be upheld by the State. Diversity at first was stoutly resisted by all rulers and conceded at last only as the alternative to chaos. Often, without too much personal conviction, the ruler determined to make the religion of the majority, however slight, the religion of the land. That is why in France the failure of Protestantism to achieve a preponderance of the entire population led eventually to the expulsion of the Huguenots. In other words, the alignment is not altogether to be attributed to differences between the Teutonic and the Latin temperament, but rather to a momentary balance of the parties at the juncture when the civil power applied its weight. The outcome, however, cannot be denied. Latin Europe is, to this day, at least ostensibly Catholic, and Northern Europe is prevailingly Protestant.

**Luther's Religious Upheaval.** But Martin Luther did not rebel because he was a German. Nor did he rebel because he was a sectary. Early in his career he

would have been ready to apply a fagot to the stake of
John Hus. He was, indeed, trained in the philosophy of
the Modernists, but imbibed from it little of that theory
of individualism which reduced Church and State to
individual components. Luther's individualism was religious. It meant that he, Martin Luther, must confront
God for himself alone.

The problem of his personal salvation obsessed him,
and he was to become a rebel only because he found
and declared the Church's way of salvation to be vain.
He had been reared in the piety of the late Middle Ages
preoccupied with the art of dying. The Church played
alternately upon fear and hope. God was popularly displayed not as a loving Father but as a terrifying Judge,
and Christ not as a tender shepherd but as the Great
Avenger. The role of compassion was assigned rather to
the Virgin Mary and the saints. Their favor must be won
by doing them honor. There was, however, much that
the suppliant could do for himself, and nothing was more
effective than to take the cowl. Under the impact of such
convictions Luther, terrified by a sudden thunder squall,
ejaculated a vow and became a monk. He entered the
Augustinian order. At first he experienced surcease, but
the former turmoil returned on the occasion of the saying
of his first Mass when he was stupefied by the realization
that he, a puny and sinful creature, was addressing God,
the All High and the All Holy. Luther then redoubled his
efforts at self-help by all the castigations the body could
endure. Still there was no alleviation of distress, for the
doubt ever recurred whether all that he had done could
be considered enough. (*See Reading 1, No. I.*) Others
might regard him as a saint. He could not so regard
himself. But the Church's way of salvation, like the
Gospel, is directed more to sinners than to saints, and
one of the great aids is the Sacrament of Penance con-
sisting of contrition, confession, and satisfaction. Luther
began to avail himself of confession and would confess
for six hours on end until the confessor was wearied and
half jocosely, half testily exclaimed: "If you are going
to confess so much why don't you go out and do something worth confessing such as killing your father or your
mother instead of trotting in with these dollie's sins?"
But Luther's problem was not whether his sins were big

or little but whether all had been confessed and absolved. He was greatly disconcerted to discover that the deepest sins cannot be confessed because they are not even recognized, just as David, after committing murder and adultery, was not contrite until convicted by the rebuke of the prophet. Nor can sins be cleared one by one. The very nature of man is corrupt (*see Reading 1, No. II*) and, as for satisfaction, man is incapable of doing anything satisfactory.

Then arose a still more devastating doubt, because if man's nature be corrupt, then God is responsible for what man is and does. The doctrine of predestination held that God did not intervene to prevent the entire human race from the taint of corruption through the sin of the primal ancestor, Adam. To some of his descendants was accorded release through special grace, whereas others were left to suffer the consequences of sins to which they had been driven by their very nature. By such thoughts Luther later affirmed he had been driven to the very abyss of desperation, and when told by his confessor that he need only love God he answered, on the contrary, that he hated Him.

Luther was to come into the clear through the study of the Bible. His superior assigned him to the teaching of the Bible in the University of Wittenberg in Saxony. The first lectures were on the Psalms. In keeping with his generation Luther interpreted the Psalms as a Christian book. He read into them the experience of Christ and the theology of Paul. He could not well do otherwise in the Twenty-second Psalm which contains the verse quoted by Christ upon the cross: "My God, my God, why hast Thou forsaken me?" In the lectures of 1513 Luther's comments on this passage are sparse. He was much fuller in his comment in 1519. (*See Reading 1, No. III.*) One needs, however, to regard the later and expanded account as expressing his earlier mind if one would explain his earlier behavior. Through meditation on this passage Luther came to see that Christ, though without sin, yet for us became sin, taking to himself human guilt and so identifying himself with the sinner as to feel estrangement from God. In Luther's mind Christ, the Judge, had become Christ, the Crucified. The Judge was also the Redeemer, and the God who condemns was seen to be the

God who through Christ is reconciling the world to Himself. What then is needed on the part of man is not castigations of the flesh nor enumeration of all offenses but only this: that man should believe what God has done in Christ and accept in trust, presenting no claim but simply accepting a gift. This is the view which Luther found already formulated in the Epistles of the Apostle Paul in terms of justification by faith. These words were to become the great slogan of the Reformation. (*See Reading 1, No. IVA, IVB.*)

**Luther the Reformer.**   These insights did not, at first, make Luther a rebel. At the outset he contemplated no reformation other than that of theological education in which the Bible should be the staple. But particular circumstances alerted him to the discrepancy between justification by faith and the current practice of the Church in the matter of indulgences. Luther, in the meantime, had become not only a professor but also a parish priest with the responsibility of the cure of souls. His parishioners were securing indulgences. The immediate occasion arose from the efforts of a prince of the House of Hohenzollern to control ecclesiastical Germany and thus to counter the power of the Hapsburgs. Albert of Hohenzollern, when not old enough to be a bishop at all, held already the sees of Halberstadt and Magdeburg. He craved, in addition, the lately vacant see of Mainz which carried with it the primacy of the Church in Germany. A huge installation fee was demanded by the Pope as well for the irregularity of such flagrant pluralism. The Pope demanded 12,000 ducats for the twelve apostles. Albert offered 7,000 for the seven deadly sins. They compromised on 10,000. Albert had to borrow the money from the great banking house of Fugger. The Pope, to enable him to recover the loan, granted an indulgence in his territories, one-half to go to Albert and the other half to go to the Pope for the building of the new Basilica of St. Peter's. Albert in his *Instructions* to the vendors of indulgences omitted the sordid details and referred only to the deplorable state of the bones of the Apostles, Peter and Paul, for which a new shrine of all Christendom should be constructed. Albert topped all previous claims for indulgences by offering not only remission of penalties but also of guilt, and the indulgence would secure prefer-

ential treatment in case of sins later to be committed.
Those already in purgatory could secure release and
those who contributed on their behalf need not themselves
be contrite. The indulgence vendor, Tetzel, even went so
far as to assert that

> "as soon as the coin in the coffer rings,
> the soul from purgatory springs."

*(See Reading 2, No. I.)*

Against these *Instructions* Luther directed his *Ninety-
five Theses* which set off the Reformation. They were
posted on the door of the Castle Church at Wittenberg on
October 30, 1517. *(See Reading 2, No. II.)* Luther was
apparently, at the time, unaware of Albert's transactions
and accepted the instructions at their face value. Luther
attacked first the bleeding of the German people for a
basilica at Rome which could not minister to the spiritual
needs of Germans. Let the Pope build the basilica out of
his own inordinate resources. Second, the Pope was declared to have no jurisdiction over purgatory. He could
do no more than remit those penalties which he had himself imposed on earth. Thus far, Luther had said nothing
especially radical. All Germans would endorse the re-
monstrance against exploitation and many theologians
would agree as to the jurisdiction over purgatory. But
Luther went on to strike not at abuses but at the very
core of the doctrine when he denied the basic theory of
the treasury of the merits of the saints, the superfluous
credits acquired through extra goodness, namely, works
of supererogation. There can be no extra credits, he
asserted. No one can do enough for himself, let alone for
anyone else. There simply is no treasury of the merits
from which to make a transfer, and those who seek a
transfer and wish to have their penalties reduced prove
thereby that they are not genuinely contrite because "they
are damned who flee damnation." The theology which
Luther grasped in the course of his lectures on Romans
*(see Reading 1, No. II)* was now brought to bear with
devastating impact on this practice of the Church.

The very core of Luther's theology was involved. The
deepest difference between him and the Church was as to
the doctrine of man. According to Luther, man can do

absolutely nothing to constitute a claim upon God. The Catholic Church holds that man can do nothing apart from prevenient grace, that grace which enables him to do good works. Everything ultimately, therefore, comes back to God. Nevertheless, given prevenient grace, man can do that which God will take into account. This Luther flatly denied, which is not to say that Luther considered man incapable of any good. Particularly in the sphere of family and civil relations man can be honorable and upright. But all of this constitutes no claim upon God. Every human action falls short in some respect in His sight, and man's only hope lies in the divine mercy. Morality in consequence is grounded not in the hope of reward but in gratitude and devotion. (*See Reading 3, No. II.*)

**Luther Prosecuted.**   Pope Leo X commissioned a Dominican, Sylvester Prierias, to reply to Luther. (*See Reading 2, No. III.*) In so doing he invoked the authority of the Church saying that the Church consists virtually in the Pope and representatively in the cardinals and that he who, in the matter of indulgences, denies what the Church actually does is a heretic. Luther retorted that the Church consists virtually in Christ and representatively in a council and that both a pope and a council can be wrong. Here was a denial of the doctrine not yet officially declared but already widely held of papal infallibility and of conciliar infallibility. (*See Reading 2, No. IV.*)

One would have supposed that the affair would have ended at once and Luther would have been placed under excommunication. Actually his case was to be protracted for four years. The reason was political. The papacy reduced to little more than an Italian city-state, nevertheless, aspired to be a world power and strove to play the game of balance between the European states. The three nations of England, France, and Spain were in the picture and in addition the ancient medieval institution, the Holy Roman Empire, which actually comprised mainly the German states. The post of emperor became vacant through the death of Maximilian I. The office was elective. The Pope did not wish to see it go to any of the great European monarchs, not to Henry VIII, the powerful Tudor sovereign, not to Francis I of France who menaced the papacy by way of northern Italy, and least of all to Charles of Spain who, as a Hapsburg, controlled also Austria and the Low Countries. The Pope preferred a small prince and his preference was for Frederick the Wise of Saxony who happened to be Luther's overlord.

Now, Frederick was an uncorruptible medieval ruler desirous of conforming to the will of God and the true faith. He was also a German, resolved to brook no Italian chicanery with regard to one of his subjects. Frederick was determined that Luther should have a fair hearing, the more so because he enjoyed the support of the entire University of Wittenberg. A fair hearing would be possible only on German soil. In view of the political importance of Frederick, the Pope temporized. Luther was accorded first a private hearing with Cardinal Cajetan at the Diet meeting at Augsburg, Germany, in 1518. The outcome was that when the Cardinal confronted Luther with a passage in the canon law plainly enunciating the doctrine of indulgences, Luther was driven to repudiate the passage and thereby to impugn the authority of the great legal code of the medieval Church. Even so, excommunication did not follow, and Luther the next year was suffered to debate in public with the mighty disputant, John Eck, at Leipzig in 1519, and there Luther again attacked papal and conciliar authority and asserted the sole authority of Scripture. He was jockeyed also into endorsing some of the views of the Bohemian sectary, John Hus. Still, excommunication did not follow.

After the election for the Empire was over and Charles of Spain had actually been chosen, because Frederick declined to vote for himself, the Pope still moved warily, and only in June of 1520 notified Luther that he must submit within sixty days. The time clock in such a case began to tick only when the summons was actually delivered, and so great was the opposition, even among German bishops, that the document was not placed in Luther's hands until October 10 of that year.

**Manifestoes of the Reform.**   In the meantime Luther busied himself bringing out some of the great manifestoes of the reform. The *Address to the Christian Nobility of the German Nation* (*see Reading 2, No. V*) dealt chiefly with the financial exactions against which the Germans had long since been issuing their *gravamina*, or complaints. The contrast resounds, so dear to the sectaries

Wyclif and Hus, between the humility and poverty of
Christ and the arrogance and pomp of the Pope. Really
more radical is the recommendation of clerical marriage.
The theory of Church-State relations in this tract evidences some ambiguity and has been the subject of debate. One recalls that the appeal is addressed to the ruling
class in Germany, including the emperor. In other words,
the civil power is called upon to implement the reforms
in the external structure of the Church. In one breath
Luther appeals to them on the ground that they are
baptized and therefore members of a Christian society.
This recalls the view of the Middle Ages that all inhabitants are citizens by birth and Christians by baptism at
birth. The whole society is therefore Christian, and in
consequence the magistrate is responsible for religion.
But in another breath Luther speaks of the rulers as
fellow believers and fellow spirituals. He seems to imply
that they may act not because they are born Christians
but because they are convinced Christians.

The distinction later became quite important when the
Lutheran churches were established by the State, and in
the modern period controlled by rulers not always conspicuous for Christian persuasion. Such a situation was
never so much as glimpsed by Luther. He was thinking in
terms of the medieval Christian society where the ruler
was deemed and commonly deemed himself to be a Christian prince responsible for the eternal salvation of his
subjects. Furthermore, Luther assumed that the Christian
nobility of the German nation were persuaded of the
truth of his Gospel. He soon discovered the contrary,
and later in his tract on *Civil Government and How Far
It Is To Be Obeyed* he sharply restricted the sphere of
government to matters temporal, the reason being that at
that time the emperor was endeavoring to suppress
Luther's translation of the New Testament. Later in
1527 when the local Lutheran princes were ready to
assist in the ecclesiastical organization, Luther did not
repulse their assistance, and a precedent was thus given
for the later Lutheran state church.

Shortly after the *Address to the Nobility* came the tract
on the sacraments entitled *The Babylonian Captivity*, so
called because Luther held the sacraments to have been
taken captive by error and abuse. (*See Reading 3.*) This

pamphlet was vastly more radical than the preceding. In fact, when Erasmus saw it, he declared the breach with Rome to be irreparable. Discussion was indeed possible as to the wealth of the Church, the income of the Cardinals, the pomp of the Curia, and even as to whether the temporal goods of the Church should be managed by national churches. Even clerical marriage was not an absolute, and the Roman Catholic church today permits it to the clergy of the Uniat churches, i.e., Eastern churches reunited with Rome by virtue of certain concessions. But the doctrine of the Sacraments does not admit of discussion. The number seven had already become fixed. The doctrine of baptism was fixed. The doctrine of the Mass was fixed. The doctrine of transubstantiation had been declared alike by a pope and a general council.

Luther, however, reduced the number of the sacraments from seven to two, namely, baptism and the Lord's Supper. His point was that a sacrament must have a visible sign of an invisible grace. In baptism the sign is water; in the Lord's Supper, bread and wine. Further, a Christian sacrament must have been instituted by Christ and must be valid solely for Christians. For this reason he rejected marriage as a sacrament on the ground that it is valid also for the Turks and the Jews. His most radical changes were as to the theory of the Mass. He denied that it is a sacrifice. He denied transubstantiation. The objection to the doctrine was that it is nowhere formulated in Scripture but is, in fact, a scholastic sophistication. To suppose that accidents can remain unaltered while substance is changed does not make any sense. This objection of itself would not be decisive because, according to Luther, when God speaks, reason must be silent; but in this instance God has not spoken and man should not introduce needless irrationalities. The doctrine of transubstantiation is not required to explain the words, "This is my body." They certainly mean that the bread and wine are the body of Christ. But this does not require an annihilation of the substance of bread and wine. As a matter of fact, Christ as God is everywhere and in everything without destroying natural substance. How this can be, we do not understand. The best we can say is that the body of Christ is in, with, and under the elements of bread and wine. But if Christ is everywhere, the question then arises why he is present in any special sense in the sacrament? The answer is that the unique quality of Christ's presence is rather at the point of man's understanding. The eyes of man are so holden that he does not see God where He is. Therefore, special channels of communication have been ordained. One is the preaching of the Word; another the administration of the sacrament. And where these two are done, there is the Church. (*Compare Reading 9, No. I, Art. 7.*) No more of a miracle takes place in one case than in the other, and the minister is simply an agent in the self-disclosure of God and does no more in the administration of the elements than in the reading of the Word, and what the minister does any Christian may do for another, though none should assume the office without a commission. Even so, the unique position of the priest is undercut, the more so because ordination was declared by Luther to be not a sacrament but only a rite of the Church. Luther's theology nullified the sacerdotalism of the Catholic Church and rendered impossible the papal theocracy based upon the unique role of the priest as one who alone can generate men to eternal life.

The Ban at Worms.    In view of such devastating onslaughts one can only marvel that Luther's excommunication was so long retarded. The sixty days allowed him by the bull expired on December 10. On that day he burned the bull together with the entire canon law. One would naturally assume that he would then automatically be under excommunication and, indeed, on January 3, 1521, the Pope issued a bull declaring that the terminus had been exceeded. Nevertheless, there was still delay because the sentence had to be executed. The bull of excommunication must be delivered to the bishops, who, by the ringing of bells and the throwing down of lighted tapers, would proclaim Luther under the ban. This step was not taken until the fall of 1521, and in consequence Luther was placed under the ban of the Empire before he had actually been excommunicated by the Church. Once more politics intervened.

Frederick the Wise was determined to have a fair hearing for his professor. A Diet of the Empire was about to meet in the city of Worms in 1521. Frederick secured from the Emperor a promise that Luther would be heard before the Diet. The promise was made, rescinded, and renewed. Three parties were exerting pressures. There were ardent followers of Luther, German nationalists armed and able to descend upon the city of Worms. The publication of the bull against Luther was held up by the papal emissary because it named also one of these blood-curdling nationalists, Ulrich von Hutten. There were also more moderate supporters of Luther, like Frederick, concerned basically for fair play. On the opposite side were rampant papalists who desired simply that Luther be condemned with nothing more than a yes or a no as to whether he adhered to his errors. And in between was a moderate group, the followers of Erasmus, who hoped that Luther might be persuaded to renounce what he had said on the sacraments and that the other points might then be negotiated. The upshot was that Luther did come to Worms. The examiner asked him whether he acknowledged all of his books. This gave him an opportunity to disclaim *The Babylonian Captivity*, but he admitted them all. Would he then defend *all* of his teaching? To this he responded in the well-known words: "Unless I am convicted by Scripture and plain reason—I do not accept the authority of popes and councils, for they have contradicted each other—my conscience is captive to the Word of God, I cannot and I will not recant anything, for to go against conscience is neither right nor safe. God help me. Amen." An effort was then made to break him by persuasion in a committee meeting. He was urged to compromise at some point lest there be *Zwietracht, Krieg und Aufruhr*, "division, war and rebellion." Luther's answer was essentially this, that one cannot compromise with regard to that which one believes to be so.

In consequence he was placed under the ban of the Empire. (*See Reading 10, No. I.*) One observes that the Edict of Worms declared him to be more subversive of the civil than of the ecclesiastical power. The point is of interest in view of the charge often made today that Luther was subservient to the State and responsible for the development of a supine state church in Germany. The fact is rather that Luther, confronted in his own day with the charge of political subversion, retorted with characteristic gusto that no one in a thousand years had so defended the civil power as he, meaning thereby that

he had defended it from papal interference. Such utterances have been misconstrued in our day to mean that he
would have endorsed the control of the Church by a
totalitarian and secularized state.

The condemnation at Worms divides Luther's career.
He was now under the ban of the Empire and shortly
to be under the ban of the Church. If apprehended at that
moment he would have been burned. His life was saved
because Frederick the Wise arranged to have him hidden
in the Castle of the Wartburg. Then began the constructive phase of Luther's work as a reformer. In his exile he
turned his religious and linguistic genius to the rendering
of the New Testament into German. The task was com-
pleted in three months. He was engaged in revision for
another quarter of a century and later also did the Old
Testament. The translation was an achievement which
no foreigner can properly appreciate. And if today a
German says that a passage in Luther's Bible is not so
very remarkable because that is the way in which any
German would say it, the answer is that any German
would say it in this way precisely because Luther so
wrote it. Not only is the work a monument of the German tongue, it is also a great book of religion. Many
passages pulsate with the life of one who for himself
could say, "out of the depths have I cried unto Thee,"
and having experienced deliverance could exclaim, "My
soul doth magnify the Lord."

**The Constructive Reformer.** After a year Luther
was called home to Wittenberg by the town council and
came in opposition to the wishes of Frederick who
warned him that were he to come into the open he could
not be protected. Luther answered that, by his prayers, he
could do more to protect Frederick than the latter by his
sword to protect Luther. The actual implementation of
the reform at Wittenberg was proving to be the occasion
of disorders. Of many of the reforms in themselves Luther
heartily approved, but not of the violence with which they
were introduced. He wished to see the Mass reformed.
Both the bread and wine should be given to the laity as
was done among the Hussites. The language of sacrifice
should be removed from the liturgy. Priests should be at
liberty to marry, and even monks and nuns. On this point,
Luther was at first somewhat hesitant and, when Melan-

chthon asked his view, ejaculated, "Anyway they will not give me a wife." But searching the Scriptures he found no warrant for monastic vows. So far, then, he endorsed the reforms but insisted that priests were not to be torn from the altars by the hair which ringed their tonsures. Luther came home, therefore, to establish order and preach moderation, reminding the people that because one can go wrong with wine and women there is no reason to prohibit wine or abolish women.

Other reforms instituted by his colleagues and agitated after his return did not meet with his approval. His colleague, Carlstadt, was an incipient Puritan who felt that the physical, the sensory, is an impediment to the life of the spirit and should be discarded. He was for smashing all of the images in the churches including the crucifixes. Music likewise he held to be a disconcerting titillation. As for the sacraments, they might be retained because of the institution of Christ, but the words "This is my body" were to be taken figuratively and no importance was to be attached to the elements as such because "the flesh profiteth nothing." Carlstadt deduced a complete social equalitarianism from the priesthood of all believers. The minister, he held, should have no academic degrees and no titles. For himself Carlstadt wished to be called simply *Bruder Andreas*. Even more, a minister should have no stipend but should work with his hands. Carlstadt took a farm. To Luther this whole program presaged the end of a learned and official ministry. Carlstadt was banished from Saxony. (*See Reading 4, Nos. I, II, and V.*)

The reason, however, was partly that he was associated, albeit incorrectly, with another man of a much more radical temper, namely, Thomas Müntzer, in whom reappeared many of the elements of the old medieval sectarianism. Müntzer believed in the speedy coming of the Lord. So, for that matter, did Luther, but Müntzer held that at his coming the ungodly must be rooted out by the angels and the angels he identified with the saints, i.e., the elect here and now. The visible Church consists of the elect who can be identified, a claim utterly repugnant to Luther. Müntzer held that a new birth in the spirit, a definite, datable, and highly emotional conversion is the proof of election. The elect then can recognize each other and form an association, a *Bund* or covenant. To them is given the kingdom, and with the sword they are to usher in the great day of the Lord. In other words, here one has the basis for a Protestant theocracy based not on sacerdotalism but on election. Incidentally, Müntzer rejected infant baptism because the evidences of election are discernible only in adults, but he did not baptize the elect because outward rites are indifferent. Here we have an intensely spiritual religion combined with eschatology and revolution. Certain aspects of Müntzer's position were to recur in Anabaptism and again in the Puritan Revolution in England. He was especially dangerous because his emergence coincided with the outbreak of the Peasant's War and without him there might well have been no uprising in Luther's Saxony. (*See Reading 4, Nos. III and IV.*)

Luther regarded him as the very arm of Satan because, under no circumstances, should violence be used on behalf of the Gospel. In any case, the elect cannot be known, and if they could, they should not undertake to establish a kingdom and to rule the world. Society cannot be properly organized on a theocratic pattern. Instead there are two kingdoms to which correspond roughly Church and State, and their spheres are distinct. As for the peasants they are wrong, no matter how much they may be right. Whatever the justice of their cause they should not as commoners take the sword into their own hands, for it is committed only to the magistrates. The common man should pray and appeal to the overlord of his oppressor. If nothing then is done, the only recourse is to wait in patience until the Lord vindicates His own. Rebellion can issue only in chaos and cannot achieve justice. Luther, with these views, could only regard the capture and execution of Müntzer in the Peasant's War as a veritable judgment of God.

In the midst of these disorders Luther married. He had intended nothing of the sort, but under the influence of his teaching, nuns left the cloister and arrived in Wittenberg. Luther undertook to find homes or husbands and succeeded until one only was left, Katherine von Bora. She intimated that she would consider Luther. He decided in favor because his parents would be pleased, the pope would be displeased, and since the Lord would soon come, there might not be another opportunity. The marriage made Luther the founder of the Protestant ministerial home which has contributed so many men of integrity and distinction to service in Church, State, the arts and sciences.

The disorders necessitated swift measures at reorganization. Luther composed sermons as models for his preachers, wrote two catechisms as an epitome of Christian teaching, one for adults and one for children, composed and compiled a hymn book. The great battle hymn of the Reformation, "A Mighty Fortress Is Our God," is his, both as to the words and music. His biblical commentaries were voluminous, strewn with passages of amazing profundity and power.

He was to continue at Wittenberg until his death in 1546. The reason that he was suffered to live so long was that the Emperor was too busy fighting the French, the Pope, and the Turks to give undivided or continuous attention to Germany. Luther, to his own acute distress, lived to die in bed while others laid down their lives for the Gospel he proclaimed.

— 3 —

# THE REFORMED CHURCHES: ZWINGLI AND THE ANABAPTISTS

Coincidentally, reform movements sprang up in other localities and, in large part, independently of Luther. The varieties of Protestantism thus are not due simply to ramifications from a single stem but to the concurrent

correction of widespread abuses. These reform movements have a great deal in common. All of the so-called
Protestants agreed with Luther in reducing the sacraments to two, in denying that the Mass is a sacrifice, and
in rejecting transubstantiation. They accepted justification by faith, the priesthood of all believers, the marriage
of the clergy, and rejected monasticism. Since so much
was held in common, to stress the differences may be
misleading. Yet if one is to describe varieties they must
be differentiated. *can & should read Bible for yourself*

**Zwingli: the Reformer of German Switzerland**
The term "Reformed" is applied to the churches of *rejected*
Switzerland both German and French, the followers of *the authority*
Zwingli and of Calvin. The implication appears to be that *of the Pope*
they were reforming Lutheranism. Actually they were like
Lutheranism combating Rome, but in many respects they
did go further than Luther, and the term "Reformed" is
not altogether inappropriate for the reform of the Reformation.

Zwingli is the great reformer of German Switzerland.
He insisted that he had not learned a single idea from
Luther, and one can understand why. He had been
trained in Humanist scholarship, and when the New
Testament of Erasmus was issued in Greek in 1516,
Zwingli memorized in the original all of the Pauline
Epistles. Anyone who knew Paul so well would not find
any new ideas in Luther. Zwingli averred that what he
did learn was the courage to do what he had already
come to believe.

He was very much more of a Humanist than Luther,
which means that he was actuated more by regard for
the authority of ancient documents than by personal
religious upheaval. For Zwingli the New Testament and
also the Old Testament were patterns for the Christian
forms of society, and he allowed much less latitude in
application than did Luther who would suffer what the
Bible did not prohibit, whereas Zwingli would endorse
only what the Bible specifically enjoined. Significantly,
Luther's first innovation was an attack on the theory that
man has any merits to present to God. The distinctive
note in Zwingli's first ministry was that he preached from
the Gospel of Matthew, following not the excerpts prescribed according to the Christian year but expounding

the entire text and doing so from the original Greek in the pulpit. This was Humanist exegesis. His concern for the translation of the Bible was no less than that of Luther, and whereas Luther was the first to bring out the New Testament in German, the Swiss anticipated him for the entire Bible, both the Old and the New, in the Zürich dialect.

Zwingli's resolve to obey the commands of Scripture led to an attack upon the dietary regulations of the Catholic Church for fast days and particularly for Lent. Not only are such regulations not enjoined in the New Testament, but they strongly resemble the Jewish food laws which the Apostle Paul so condemned. (*See Reading 5, No. I.*) Zwingli's followers began to eat meat during Lent. Froschauer, the printer at Zürich, justified himself on the ground that he needed strength to bring out the New Testament by Easter.

Then came an attack on images in the churches, the statues of the saints and even the crucifix. All of this was reminiscent of Carlstadt who had found a refuge in Switzerland. The text adduced was: "Thou shalt not make unto thee any graven image." Like Carlstadt, Zwingli also rejected music in the churches, the more surprisingly because he himself was an accomplished musician on some half dozen instruments. But he held that music is for private relaxation and not for the worship of God. Again he agreed with Carlstadt that the words of institution for the Lord's Supper, "This is my body," are to be taken only spiritually. (*See Reading 5, No. IV.*) Curiously the text against images was taken literally; the text on the body and blood, spiritually. One suspects something deeper here than mere Biblicism. What holds together these three points—the rejection of images, music, and sacramentalism—is an aversion to the external and physical as a proper medium for divine communication on the ground that God is a spirit and must be worshipped in spirit and that "the flesh profiteth nothing." One marvels that Zwingli kept the sacraments at all. A century later the Quakers were to reject them in any external sense. There is in Zwingli an inheritance from the mystical tradition of the late Middle Ages transmitted through Erasmus who had been reared by the Brethren of the Common Life and had learned to decry all relics, pilgrimages, and even sacraments as *external.* "What matters," said he, "is not a relic of Paul but the spirit of his teaching."

Zwingli retained the sacraments only by denuding them of their meaning. The Lord's Supper he regarded as a memorial of Christ's death, though later in life he would concede that there might also be a communion with His spirit. Participation in the Supper does more, however, to benefit those who see it taken than those who receive, because to take it in the presence of a congregation is to give a public testimonial and to strengthen the faith of the witnesses. Baptism, on that score, would appear to be less defensible, but Zwingli retained it even for babies on the ground that the Church is the company of the elect and the successor to ancient Israel, and as under the old dispensation children were held to belong and were initiated by circumcision, so under the new dispensation they are sealed with baptism in the hope, of course, that they will subsequently confirm the vows taken on their behalf. (*See Reading 5, Nos. II and III.*)

Here is a further development of the idea of a Protestant theocracy centering around an elect people. There is still the question of how the elect are to be identified. The mark for Zwingli was faith. (*See Reading 5, No. V.*) On that basis not all of the people in Zürich could be regarded precisely as the elect. Some Catholics were still allowed to reside, although not to participate in public affairs. Zwingli freely admitted that the Church cannot be held to consist only of the elect. It is a mixed body composed of wheat and also tares. Yet circumstances aided the process of weeding, for such pressures of a military character were exerted against Zürich by the Catholic cantons that merely to remain in the city was an act of courage and a testimony of faith. Increasingly Zürich assumed the form of a chosen people, the elect of the Lord, striving for themselves and their children to achieve under God a holy commonwealth. This idea was to have profound influence in New England by way of English Puritanism which, at many points, was more influenced by Zürich than by Geneva.

**Anabaptism.** In the circle of Zwingli at Zürich, as earlier in the circle of Luther at Wittenberg, arose a more radical movement. The two were not unrelated, and the radicals at Zürich wrote to Carlstadt and Müntzer hailing them as the best exponents of the Gospel in their generation, although the violence of Müntzer was explicitly repudiated. The group at Zürich came to be called Anabaptists. The word is derived from the Greek and means "to baptize again." It was applied to this group because they rejected infant baptism and conferred the rite upon adults, even though they had already been baptized as babies. Opponents called this a repetition of baptism, but this the Anabaptists denied on the ground that the dipping of children is not baptism at all and worth no more than "ducking in a cow trough." The only valid baptism is that which follows an inward experience of regeneration, a dying to Christ and rising with him in newness of life. This experience is possible only for adults. These sectaries, therefore, wished to be called not Anabaptists but simply Baptists.

The movement was eventually to attain a remarkable cohesion, but at the outset was very fluid and not sharply differentiated from a welter of ecstatic vagaries which revived, without direct borrowing, the main themes of medieval sectarianism. There were chiliasts who looked for the immediate inauguration of the thousand-year reign of Christ, revolutionaries like Müntzer who would usher it in with the sword, quietists who would leave all to the hand of the Lord, spirit-filled prophets who claimed to speak with as much authority as the prophets of old, divinely chosen leaders who looked upon themselves as new Enochs and Elijahs, the two figures who, according to ancient prophecy, should reappear to presage the coming of Messiah. There were Biblical literalists who took the Sermon on the Mount to the letter and set it decisively over against the Old Testament with its chronicles of the wars of the Lord. And there were Old Testament literalists who revived polygamy and crusades and imitated some of the eccentricities of the prophets. Controversies ensued over personal claims as well as over the inner versus the outer word of Scripture. Some so pressed the inner that the outer became only an allegory, and even the whole historic drama of redemption in Christ was reduced to a symbol of that which must take place in the inner life of the believer. All save a handful were agreed that the true Church is bound to be small and persecuted, that it cannot be affiliated with the State which embraces all of the inhabitants of an unpurged community. The Church must be pure, continually purified by banning the unworthy and consequently becoming a select, voluntary society.

To find a name to describe such diversified developments is not easy. If the whole movement be called Anabaptist, then radical differentiation must be recognized within Anabaptism. Another and broader terminology was suggested by Luther when he said that he had taken the middle way between the Catholics to the left and the radicals to the right. In modern parliamentary parlance these directions have been reversed, and we now use the left for the radical. In this sense we can talk of the left-wing of the Reformation. Yet what the body was to which the wings were attached must still be precisely demarcated.

Luther assigned to what he called the left not only the Wittenberg radicals and the Anabaptists but Zwingli as well, yet Zwingli persecuted the Anabaptists. A convenient, though arbitrary, classification places the Catholics on the right, with their sacramental hierarchical system and union of Church and State. In the middle are those Protestant groups which retained the Church-State relationship, namely, Luther, Zwingli, the Anglicans, and Calvin. To the left are all of the others, i.e., the Anabaptists in the narrower sense together with spiritual reformers, some of whom went so far as to dissolve the very notion of the Church, and the revolutionaries who made the Kingdom of God a thing of the here and now.

The Anabaptists at Zürich, Grebel, and Manz were Humanists and patricians. The assumption that Anabaptism was a movement of the disinherited certainly does not fit the beginnings. One of their own historians has neatly said that the Anabaptists were not Anabaptists because they were disinherited. They were disinherited because they were Anabaptists. These young men shared Zwingli's conviction that the Bible offers a pattern for the Church and with him earnestly searched the Scriptures, finding there no example and no warrant for infant baptism. Zwingli agreed, and he might have been willing to take the appropriate steps of dropping it entirely had he

not speedily become aware of far-reaching implications,
because infant baptism goes with a theory of the Church
as co-terminus with the community and affiliated with
all of its institutions, particularly the State. When all of
the children are baptized and are considered therefore to
be, in some sense, Christians, one may regard every in-
habitant as Christian, and the institutions such as the
school and the State which embrace the entire community
may be regarded as only different branches along with
the Church in the administration of a Christian commonwealth. But if the Church were to be comprised only of
those who had had a heartfelt experience of grace as the
prerequisite for baptism and who gave evidence of conversion by a godly deportment and if all others were to
be excluded by the ban, then the Church would become
a conventicle comparatively small, certainly not embracing the entire populace and in consequence not to
be equated with the State. The only way then to combine
Church and State would be to exclude the unqualified
from both institutions, in which case Church and State
might be one but both would be distinguished from the
community. This later was done in the New England
colonies. Zwingli's position was more selective than that
of the Church of the Middle Ages and less than that of
Calvinist New England. As already observed he desired a
purge of the Church and circumstances effected a weeding at Zürich, but he did not propose to go so far as to
make of the Church an association of the twice born only
and to exclude the children. To do this would be to renounce the pattern of the new Israel of God.

Even less was he inclined to concur when he discovered that the Anabaptists proposed not merely to dissolve
the alliance of Church and State but to disintegrate the
State itself. In their judgment the Christian should not
use a sword either on his own behalf or on behalf of
another. To be sure, they conceded, the State is ordained of God as Paul said, but it is ordained because of
unbelievers and its administration should be left to unbelievers. The Christian should not be a magistrate.
Moreover, the Anabaptists would not take an oath on
which in that day so many civil institutions were made to
rest. (*See Reading 5, Nos. VI-XI.*)

   **Persecution of Anabaptists.** All of this might perhaps have been tolerated by Zwingli had the Anabaptists been few and docile, but they waxed strong and raved. They were vociferous and dramatic missionaries. In a neighboring village two men in ordinary garb came to the village fountain where the animals drank, and there one baptized the other. An Anabaptist preacher in the midst of a church service called out against the minister and, on another occasion, arrived first and was haranguing the people when the appointed pastor arrived. Every Anabaptist man or woman was expected to go out on missionary tours.

Zürich first resorted to banishment, but this did no good. Other cities sent them back, and in any case the Anabaptists would not stay away. Philip of Hesse, the only Protestant prince who refused to resort to extreme measures, found the Anabaptists exceedingly vexing. No matter how frequently banished, they felt an especial call to return and testify. Imprisonment was the next recourse, and in prison interminable disputations were conducted by the ministers. Zürich had not so much patience, and in 1526 an ancient law of the code of Justinian was revived which visited on certain ancient disorderly sectaries, who refused to recognize Catholic baptism, the penalty of death because of their repetition of the rite. Under this old so-called Roman law, Felix Manz was drowned in the Lake of Zürich. Grebel died of the plague. The outstanding leaders of the movement in the next decade were plucked by drowning, fire, or gallows. In 1529 at the Diet of Speier the Anabaptists were placed under the penalty of death for the entire empire. Catholics and Lutherans concurred.

Then less balanced spirits came to the fore, the new Enochs and Elijahs, the chiliasts, the imitators of prophetic eccentricities, and in the town of Münster in 1534 the Anabaptists succeeded in taking over the government. A sudden revelation led to the abandonment of pacificism, and a reign of the saints was instituted after Old Testament models with the introduction of polygamy. Catholics and Lutherans united to suppress the saints. The whole episode gave to Anabaptism an unsavory name but did not extinguish the movement.

The sober and sobered remnants were gathered up by Menno Simons in Holland and Jacob Hutter in Moravia.

Polygamy, chiliasm, messianism, pretensions to dreams, and special revelations were repudiated in favor of a religion highly ethical, disciplined, austere if not ascetic, renouncing luxury, license and the protection of the sword. The communities were dedicated to suffering in obedience to their suffering Lord. (*See Reading 5, Nos. X and XI.*)

Menno Simons and Jacob Hutter were confronted by a stupendous task to weld communities out of irrepressible nonconformists. The Anabaptist missionaries and martyrs were superb obstructionists, denouncing the ministers and the magistrates, uncowed by any danger, invincible in disputation, unconquerable under torture, invincible in death. How could such people learn to live with each other? They were committed to striving for perfection and were resolved to use the ban against any defections from their stringent regulations. The Hutterites practiced communal living with a sharing of all goods. When a dispute had already arisen between two "shepherds," the wife of one was discovered to have secreted a pair of private underwear and five gold guldin. She was, therefore, a Sapphira. Her husband was found to be privy to her crime. He was an Ananias. A schism ensued. Nevertheless, in time the irenic spirit and statesman-like qualities of Menno and Hutter did weld communities which have survived and largely maintained their pattern through these 400 years.

They were able to survive only by accommodation or migration, or perhaps both, as in the case of the Mennonites. Those who remained in Holland somewhat tempered their regime. Others moved to the east of Europe. The Hutterites took advantage of the feudal structure on the eastern fringes of the empire to accept asylum on the estate of a nobleman in Moravia. When the emperor threatened to intervene, this nobleman replied that he would defend these poor folk with the sword, but they declined to be defended and took to their wagons until they found a prince who agreed both to tolerate and not to protect. Then came the golden interlude. When later pressures were applied, some secured immunity by accepting the Catholic mass with a proviso that they might retain their way of life which, after all, did not greatly differ from Catholic monasticism. Others went to Russia where also many of the Mennonites had flown. When, in the late nineteenth century, persecution broke out in that area, many migrations took place to Canada and to the Midwest of the United States. Some colonies are in the Far West. Recently the Hutterites have experienced a revival in England and Paraguay, and a *Bruderhof* has been established in New York. The ancient pattern is preserved by isolation, aided by distinctive dress and speech. Within the confines of the Brotherhood, plain frocks and radiant faces bespeak a people at peace.

— 4 —

# CALVINISM

Calvinism was another branch of the church called Reformed. It was activist, exceeding the other varieties of Protestantism, and it was the most international. Although Zwinglianism greatly affected English Puritanism, Calvinism supplied the theology and Calvinism was the form of Protestantism which took hold in France, the Netherlands, Scotland, and New England. Many of the ingredients of the American concept of life are a heritage from Calvinism, and it is not by accident that one of our presidents was called Calvin Coolidge.

**Calvin on God and the Church.** John Calvin was a young refugee for religion from France who, at Basel in 1536, came to public notice through the publication of his *Institutes of the Christian Religion,* the most outstanding and influential systematic formulation of Protestant teaching. When it was written, the main lines between Catholics and Protestants and between Protestant varieties were already clearly and sharply drawn. The Augsburg Confession in 1530 had already offered a brief exposition of Protestant teaching. (*See Reading 9, No. I.*) The death penalty had been imposed the year previously upon the Anabaptists throughout the empire. The Roman Inquisition was, to be sure, as yet four years in the offing, but the stand of the Catholic Church could not be mistaken. As the Protestants became more entrenched, the Catholics became more intransigent. These attitudes were already matured when Calvin wrote. That is why he had no tentative and tolerant period. He emerged chipped from flint, and the dedication of his *Institutes* to Francis I, the King of France, was no mincing feeler. He told the king roundly that Protestant teaching was nothing other than the Gospel of Jesus Christ (*see Reading 6, No. II*), and the king would do well to heed and follow if he would rule his country with tranquillity. John Calvin was a little naive, however, in disclaiming any revolutionary implication in the new teaching. He was quite right that the Huguenots, as Protestants were called in France, were engaged in no subversive political propaganda, but he was a trifle obtuse not to perceive that in a land where Catholicism was deemed to be the one true faith and the State was intimately linked with the Church, a change in religion was bound also to affect the State.

The differences between Calvinism and Lutheranism are greater than those between Calvin and Luther. On all the main points the two were agreed. Even on the Lord's Supper Calvin's readiness to accept a real, albeit a spiritual, presence was less objectionable to Luther than Zwingli's memorial theory. (*See Reading 6, No. III.*) Nevertheless, there were variant emphases. Luther's theology has been compared to a flower all the petals of which are attached as a center to the forgiveness of sins. Calvin's center was the sovereignty of God. (*See Reading 6, No. II.*) He commenced his *Institutes* not with justification by faith but with the knowledge of God. Calvin was overwhelmed by the sense of the majesty of God who sits above the circle of the earth, before whom the nations are as a drop in the bucket, who exalts and abases, who is the Lord of time, the director of history, the end and aim of man's endeavor and aspiration. If Anabaptism has rightly been called the Gospel of utter obedience, the same might equally be said of

Calvinism, except that for the Anabaptist the obedience was directed to Christ and for Calvin to God.

The chief end of man is to glorify God and not to save oneself. When Cardinal Sadoleto, the Catholic Bishop of Geneva, sought to recall his parishioners by telling them they had a better chance in Catholicism of salvation, Calvin retorted that such a consideration was altogether unworthy. (*See Reading 6, No. IV.*) Man's chief concern is not his own salvation but to fulfill the commands and exalt the name of God. Tacitly, this was a rebuke also to Luther whose very rebellion originated in an anguished concern as to his own status with God. Calvin believed that no one could worship God aright who was everlastingly worried about his salvation. If one were to accept and practice Calvin's attitude, plainly enormous resources of energy would be released for other modes of activity.

Calvin knew where and how to put these resources to work. He believed that God had a great plan for the ages. The sovereign Lord, who with an outstretched arm brought the children of Israel up out of Egypt and led them through the Wilderness into the Land of Promise, having rejected ancient Israel because of apostasy, had constituted a new Israel in the Christian Church. This was already the concept of Zwingli, but Calvin conceived of the scope of this new Israel as extending far beyond the confines of a Swiss city. And he had a somewhat different picture of how it was constituted. The new Israel is made up of the elect, but how are they to be known? Calvin, like Zwingli, answered that they cannot be perfectly known, yet there are presumptive tests. For Zwingli the mark was faith. Calvin added two more indications. One was an upright life. Here he was in accord with the Anabaptists. Curiously, he did not include an experience of the new birth with a highly emotional accompaniment as did Müntzer and later the New England Calvinists. The third test for Calvin was participation in the sacraments. He, then, who has the faith and life, and shows his love by coming to the Lord's table, is presumably of the elect. (*See Reading 6, No. V.*) ..

The Church can be made to consist only approximately of the elect, and the Anabaptist claim that the tares can be altogether weeded from the vineyard of the Lord was

rejected. At the same time Calvin also used the ban almost as rigorously as they. He was, above all, insistent
that the ban should be controlled only by the Church
and not by the State. This is the more remarkable because he demanded that the State also be manned by
the godly. Nevertheless, there is a distinction of function, and church discipline belongs to the Church. On
this score he once suffered banishment and almost again,
but the government in the end conceded his demands,
and excommunication thereafter was vested solely in the
consistory, a purely ecclesiastical body.

But while insisting on a church at least relatively pure
and approximately of the chosen, Calvin at the same
time equated the Church with the entire community in
Geneva. He who was within the town was also within
the Church. This could be only if he who was not within
the Church was not suffered to remain within the town,
and roughly that is what happened. The ban from the
Church did not entail automatically banishment from
the city, but one who remained under excommunication
for a length of time could scarcely expect to reside indefinitely within the walls.

Circumstances aided Calvin even more than Zwingli
because Geneva was begirt by foes. The city was situated
on the apex of a triangle jutting into Catholic France,
with Italy not far removed. There was constant danger
during Calvin's lifetime that the former ruler of the city,
the Duke of Savoy, or, for that matter, the King of
France or the Duke of Alva on his way from Spain to
the Netherlands might attack. And after Calvin's death
there was an attempt to scale the walls. In consequence,
a selective process affected the population. All Catholics
who would not accept the new regime had left even
before Calvin's arrival. During his stay some 6,000
refugees for the Reformed faith were added to an
original population of 13,000. Thus by withdrawals and
additions Geneva became well nigh as select as a Hutterian colony.

Here is a fine example of the combination of the church
comprehensive and the sect rigoristic. The combination is
effected by a Protestant theocracy in which all of the
populace is dedicated to showing forth the glory of God,
in which the magistrates no less than the ministers con-

ceive of themselves as servants of the holy commonwealth, in which jurisdiction over heresy, if not over moral
discipline, was left to the town council, and the syndics
were no less saints, competent to expound and apply the
Word of God.

The teachers in this theocracy were given an exalted
place. Here medieval tradition was preserved, for in the
Middle Ages Church, State, and School were considered
the three prime institutions in Christendom. In Geneva
the terminology only was altered to Church, State, and
Academy. Calvin himself was both preacher and teacher
and, although the schoolmaster as such was not of the
clergy, he was expected to have all of the qualifications.
Geneva became a training ground not only for youths
in elementary disciplines but for theological candidates,
who after their training were to go out as emissaries to
France, Holland, and the British Isles. Calvinism was
no less missionary than Anabaptism.

Calvin's Letters.  Calvin's letters offer an admirable
example of the extent of his influence and the character of
his counsel. (*See Reading 6, No. VI.*) There is one, for
example, to the Duke of Somerset, the Lord Protector in
England during the first three years of the reign of his
nephew, Edward VI. The Duke was one of the most tolerant princes of his age and ended, perhaps for that reason,
on the scaffold. Calvin sought to harden him to sterner
measures against the superstitions of Anti-Christ on the
one hand (Roman Catholicism), and on the other against
the fanaticism of the disorderly (by whom Calvin would
mean the Anabaptists).

A letter to a nobleman in Poland, like the dedication
to Francis I, disclaimed a responsibility for revolution
on the part of the Protestants. In this instance, Calvin
was not in a position to deny disorder. His point was
that the truth cannot be held responsible for disorder
which would not exist if truth were recognized. Those
who resist the Gospel, therefore, bear the blame, which
practically amounts to saying that, if Protestants disturb the peace, the responsibility lies with the Catholics
because they do not become Protestants. It might have
been less disingenuous to say simply that truth is more
important than peace.

At the same time, Calvin did have a very great concern

for peace and order and was extremely loath to wreck political constitutions. This is evident in his letter to Coligny where Calvin would prefer that Protestantism be extinguished than that it survive through the shedding of blood. But more on this point later.

The personal aspect of these struggles is pointedly revealed in the letter to Renée, the Duchess of Ferrara. Calvin had been a visitor at her court and had won her to his persuasion. Her position was exceedingly difficult because the Catholic duke, her husband, placed grave restrictions upon the exercise of her religion. Saddest of all was the marriage of her daughter to the Duke of Guise, the leader of the Catholic faction in France and the perpetrator of that massacre which set off the wars of religion. The Huguenots proclaimed the duke to be damned, but his mother-in-law could not bring herself to so harsh a judgment. Calvin conceded the ignorance of man as to the duke's present status, but this concession was not derived from any softness. Personal affection must not be suffered to blur the inexorable judgment of faith, and the truth of God must take precedence over all the claims of the flesh.

Calvinism, like Anabaptism, bred a race of martyrs, but unlike Anabaptism a race also of generals, men of the stamp of Coligny, William the Silent, and Oliver Cromwell. Calvinism is the finest example of what has been called "innerworldly asceticism." Here is a disciplined way of life, quite as strenuous as that of the Mennonites or the Hutterites, but not aloof from the State, and withdrawn to the frontiers of a centralized society. Calvinism did not take cover under the aegis of vestigial feudalism but struck for the rulers of the newly consolidating national monarchies. One notes how many of the letters of Calvin are to princes, and if princes were not amenable, then let them renounce their thrones on peril of their lives. Calvin was very careful to define the terms on which they might be deposed or decapitated. His followers had less qualms. Despite the disclaimer which he addressed to the King of France, Calvinism was actually the most revolutionary form of sixteenth-century Protestantism.

# — 5 —

# SCANDINAVIA AND THE BRITISH ISLES

**Sweden.** In some cases the princes were happy enough to embrace the reform for reasons of their own. The theology of John Calvin was not the driving force, nor was concern to advance the glory of God. The motive was rather to throw off the control of Rome. The new national monarchies resented the universalism of the medieval Church. Some circumvented it by nationalism within the framework of Catholicism. Such was the essence of Gallicanism in France, and a parallel movement, as we have noted, occurred in Spain. Sweden and England were to establish national churches distinct from Rome. In Sweden, including also Denmark, a Protestant national church was established in 1527. There developed a union of Church and State more intimate than any in Germany which remained confessionally as well as politically divided. At the same time the Swedish Lutheran Church maintained a greater independence with respect to the State than did the Lutheran Church at a subsequent period in Prussia or the Anglican Church where the king was the head of the Church, as he was not in Sweden.

**England.** In England a quarrel occurred with the papacy over a royal marriage. There was not much else over which it could have occurred because England had already attained independence of Rome at the point of "provisions" to English sees and appeals to Rome. Marriage remained, because marriage was a sacrament of the Church and for centuries had been subject to ecclesiastical courts. The Church allowed no divorce, but annulment on the ground of a flaw in the marriage was not too difficult to secure. Marriages, one suspects, were contracted sometimes with an eye to flaws, especially among rulers whose political constellations might call for the mating of other stars. The flexi-

53

bility was derived from the Church's prohibitions and
dispensations. Marriages were not to be contracted up to
the fifth or even the sixth degree of consaguinity, nor
with those spiritually related through having stood spon-
sor in baptism, thereby incurring a tie and an impediment
alike with the child and the relatives of the child. Yet
every impediment, except in case of close physical relationship, could be dispensed. If, later, the dispensation
were found to be defective, the marriage could be annulled, and in that case the offspring could be legitima-
tized.

This was the system of which Henry VIII desired to
take advantage. He had been married to Katherine of
Aragon at a time when England prized an alliance with
Spain. The union had produced several stillborn children
but only one survivor, and she was a girl, the Princess
Mary. A male was eminently to be desired because
England had just emerged from wars of succession and
had not yet had the experience of successful queens like
Elizabeth, Anne, and Victoria. There was grave reason
to fear that the accession of the Princess Mary might
precipitate a recurrence of disorder.

Now it happened that Katherine was the widow of
Henry's brother, Arthur, and the book of Leviticus for-
bids marriage with a deceased brother's widow (*Lev. 20,
21*). This was clearly recognized at the time, and the
Pope had then given a dispensation. What more simple
than to declare the dispensation faulty, to grant an annulment, and to free Henry for a new union! The present
Pope, Clement VII, was quite ready to negotiate, but for
years he stalled. Some think he had no alternative because in 1527 Rome was captured by the Emperor
Charles V, who was also the King of Spain and the
nephew of Katherine of Aragon. He is thought to have
prevented the Pope from compliance, but a recent
Catholic historian quotes the imperial ambassador near
the end of the proceedings as saying that he could not
predict the outcome. That might have been true, even
if he had been exerting pressure, for who could tell
whether the Pope would think it more expedient to
alienate the emperor and suffer perhaps some curtailment
of the papal states or to offend Henry and lose England
for the faith? In any case the Pope stalled.

Henry took things into his own hands. To him it would certainly appear that the Pope was playing Spanish policy and, if that were true, then the papacy was not genuinely universal, in which case a national state could not brook papal overlordship on a question affecting political succession. Henry intimidated the Pope into consecrating as Archbishop of Canterbury Thomas Cranmer, a Lutheran and he, as head of the English Church, granted a divorce. (*See Reading 7, No. I.*) The succession was fixed upon the Princess Elizabeth (a girl after all), the daughter of Anne Boleyn in default of a subsequent heir.

Then, in the year 1534, Henry established an English national church, the *Ecclesia Anglicana* with himself as the supreme head with power to "repress and extirp all errors and heresies." (*See Reading 7, No. II.*) Some have contended that this was really no innovation because, in the century following the barbarian invasions, England had been severed from the continent and the English Church had gone its own way without regulation by or recognition of Rome. True enough, but still one cannot speak at that early date of an English national church for the simple reason that there was then no English nation. Under Henry there was definitely something new.

Yet there were precedents, and the closest is to be found in the so-called Caesaro-papism of the Emperor Justinian in the Byzantine Empire. There Church and State were allied, with the State taking the lead even to the point of summoning councils, promulgating ecclesiastical legislation, and even influencing the formulation of doctrine. Never, however, was the emperor a priest, and no magistrate could perform the rites of the Church. Another parallel was to be found in the Church of the West in the Middle Ages where the empire regarded itself as the civil arm of a Christian society responsible for the structure, the integrity, the morals and sometimes even the faith of the Church. Not infrequently, a genuine concern for reform actuated the interventions of Christian rulers. The new national states claimed for themselves to be the successors of the empire, and an English king it was who said *Rex est im-*

*perator in regno suo* (Richard II), "the king is the emperor in his own domain."

The theory which justified Henry's act is called Erastianism. The word is taken from the name of an obscure Swiss theologian, Erastus. It is the doctrine that the State may determine the form of religion. This view received its most extreme formulation at the hands of Thomas Cranmer who said that the king wields two keys, i.e., both the temporal and the spiritual. On the other side, so extreme a claim had never been made by the Pope, though one of the canon lawyers had gone so far as to assert that the Church holds the two keys. The claim was now countered not by the Empire but by one of the new national states. Sir Thomas More took this to mean that the State might even abolish religion. "If Parliament should decree that there is no God, would there then be no God?" But this, of course, was not what Cranmer meant. He was thinking all along in terms of a Christian society. He deemed the State to be a Christian institution and never envisaged the possibility that the king might abrogate Christianity.

As a matter of fact, Henry abrogated very little. His one drastic act was his dissolution of the monasteries and even this was drastic only because so complete. The monasteries no longer served the same social purpose as in the Middle Ages and already their endowments were being expropriated in order to found colleges. Henry swept them largely into the coffers of the State. In consequence, few of the monastic houses are better preserved than in England, for the surest way to preserve without change is to stop using.

On the positive side, Henry introduced the Bible in the English tongue into the churches. Coverdale was commissioned to provide a translation. He availed himself largely of the work of Tyndale, which earlier in his reign Henry had been buying up for burning, and Tyndale had gladly sold in order to use the proceeds for a better edition. Poor old Tyndale, in the meantime, stayed on the continent and was burned. He might have fared no better had he returned to England during the last days of Henry, who, to allay Catholic opposition, turned savagely against Lutheran teachings and had several Lutherans burned. Coincidentally, the Catholic

Cardinal Fisher and Sir Thomas More were sent to the block.

**Edward VI and Mary.** Changes were frequent in England for the remainder of the sixteenth century and all emanated from the crown. The people were singularly quiescent. England was not aflame over religion until the century following. Under the Tudors political security and internal order were the main concern, and the vagaries and tyrannies of despots were supinely endured for the most part, so long as the brigands were off the roads and the raiders off the seas.

Henry did, in the end, have a son by Jane Seymour, who, as a mere lad of ten, succeeded to the throne in 1547 as Edward VI under the protectorate of his uncle, the Duke of Somerset to whom Calvin wrote the letter previously mentioned. The Duke, after three years, was supplanted by Warwick, the Duke of Northumberland, who was the Protector for the next three years. These two protectorates were marked by a progressively radical Protestantism. The reason was, in part, the influx of foreigners. On the continent the attempt of Charles V to enforce on the Protestants a compromise basically Catholic drove many intransigents into exile, and they entered into the councils of Archbishop Cranmer. Their influence is noticeable in the two editions of the prayer-book composed by Cranmer. This magnificent liturgy of the Church of England has done more than all else, by its stately prayers and sonorous cadences, to endear the English Church to the English people. In the first prayerbook the formula for the administration of the Lord's Supper admits of a Lutheran and possibly even a Calvinist interpretation. It is this: "The body of our Lord Jesus Christ which was given for thee preserve thy body and soul unto everlasting life." The second prayer-book was rather Zwinglian in tone and read: "Do this in remembrance that Christ died for thee and feed on Him in thy heart by faith and with thanksgiving." (*See Reading 7, No. III.*)

When Edward died at the age of sixteen in 1553, an attempt was made by Northumberland to change the succession in favor of his niece, Lady Jane Grey, but the English wanted a Tudor even though she might be a Catholic, and the Princess Mary, daughter of Katherine of Aragon, succeeded. She was married to her second cousin, Philip, the bigoted Catholic monarch of Spain. Mary restored Catholic obedience. In all, some 250 Protestant leaders were sent to the stake.

Among them was Archbishop Cranmer. His position was fraught with extreme difficulty because of his doctrine of Erastianism. He had held that the king holds the two keys, that the king may determine the form of religion for his land, but now the queen determined to return to Rome. If the head of the State might settle the form of religion, why should there not be a return to Rome?—except that such a return was to deny that the king holds the two keys. Logic and conscience were at war. Cranmer recanted, tore up his recantation, again recanted, and all of this several times. He did not thereby save himself, for he was condemned to the stake at Oxford. In his speech before the execution, he confessed that, to save his life, he had signed with his hand what he did not believe in his heart, wherefore when he came to the fire this hand should be the first to suffer.

**Elizabeth.**    Mary was succeeded by her half-sister Elizabeth, the daughter of Anne Boleyn. The queen had an eye to expediency and presumably not too much concern for the more minute differences of religion. She called it all a bagatelle. Still, her final cast for Protestantism may have been a gesture of conviction. It was not too politic in 1559. To be sure, the Lutherans on the continent had attained toleration in limited territories by the Peace of Augsburg in 1555 (*see Reading 10, No. VIII*), but wars of religion were on the point of breaking out in France. The Netherlands were not yet clearly in a position to stage a successful revolt against Spain. Scotland was independent of England and allied with Catholic France, and Spain was ruled by the bigoted Philip II. Elizabeth was courageous to repudiate the Pope.

At the same time she was of no mind to alienate Catholics in England any more than her very act necessitated. She would not harry them if they were politically loyal, nor demand of them too precisionist a conformity. (*See Reading 7, No. VII.*) Her hope was to unify England insofar as might be possible around a Protestant core with a latitudinarian fringe. Conformity was demanded primarily in externals (*see Reading 7, No. V*) and Puritans who would not comply were penalized. (*See Reading 7, No. VI.*) The Thirty-nine Articles later to be discussed (*see Reading 9, No. II*) were designed to be comprehensive. Even more, the prayerbook should enable those of differing convictions to join in common supplication about the table of the Lord. The formulae of the two Edwardian books were simply combined: "The body of our Lord Jesus Christ which was given for thee preserve thy body and soul unto everlasting life. Take this in remembrance that Christ died for thee and feed on Him in thy heart by faith and with thanksgiving."

Scotland. The Reformation in Scotland was the work of one of the most intransigent of the Calvinists, John Knox. He had served a year as a Protestant prisoner in the French galleys, and his spirit had not thereby been mellowed. In his eyes one celebration of the Mass is worse than a cup of poison. To understand language so bitter, one must bear in mind the circumstances. Knox's significant period in Scotland begins only in 1560. By that time persecution of Protestants was rampant in France, and the six years of Bloody Mary in England, in which many of his former colleagues—he had a pastorate in England—had been burned, was only just terminated. Mary had died in 1559. Rome appeared to Knox, even more than to his Protestant predecessors, as indisputably the scarlet woman seated on the seven hills and drunk with the blood of the saints.

By 1560 a strongly Protestant party had developed in Scotland. There was also a party, which if not exactly pro-English, was certainly anti-French because the French alliance had brought French troops into the land. Moreover, the Queen Regent Mary, the widow of James V, was a French woman of the house of Guise, the most Catholic house in France. She was a sister of that Duke of Guise, whom the Huguenots in France were proclaiming as damned, to the distress of the Duchess of Ferrara. Still worse, the daughter of this Mary of Guise, the Queen Regent in Scotland, was another Mary, later to be Mary Queen of Scots, and married at that time to Francis II, the King of France. The Queen Regent in Scotland concluded a treaty whereby her son-in-law, the King of France, was to become the King of Scotland. This agreement was frustrated by the death of the king.

Still the disclosure that the promise had been made greatly strengthened the anti-French party. When, then, the Queen Regent died, the Treaty of Edinburgh in 1560 decreed the expulsion of French troops and declared the celebration of the Mass to be a penal offense. Young Mary, now a widow, came back to Scotland as Queen. She had been living in France under the tutelage of her uncle, the Cardinal of Lorraine, and was of no mind to comply with the Treaty of Edinburgh. But Knox looked upon the Mass, even in the queen's private chapel, as the prelude to the reinstitution of Catholicism for all Scotland. Therefore, he was steel to her tears and was frank in telling her that princes who do not follow the truth of God cannot be endured. (*See Reading 11, No. IV.*) Of this more later. The upshot of it all was that Mary, by her follies and crimes, made herself impossible and sought asylum in England. Elizabeth took her under protective custody until plots against her own life, centering around the person of Mary, rendered her such a political menace that Parliament ordered her execution.

In Scotland in the meantime, Knox brought Calvinism to full-fledged Presbyterianism. For the first time on a national scale Calvinism was able to deploy with a system of ascending representative assemblies. The General Assembly was to rival in importance the Scottish Parliament.

The victory of Protestantism in Scotland rendered possible the union of the two kingdoms, Scotland and England. In that age a union in politics without a union in religion was unthinkable. If England had been Protestant and Scotland Catholic, they could never have come together. As it was, to unite two varieties of Protestantism, namely Presbyterianism and Anglicanism, was a great venture which succeeded only after the Puritan Revolution in which the clash of the two systems was a major ingredient.

Yet John Knox may be regarded as the tree surgeon who grafted the two growths. As for Mary, her son became James VI of Scotland and James I of England.

— 6 —

# THE CATHOLIC REFORMATION

**Reform Liberal and Stringent.** Catholic reform all
this time had not lagged. A beginning had been made
before the Protestant Reformation. In Spain Cardinal
Ximenes was a strange figure, an ardent Franciscan who
walked barefoot like Saint Francis and when commanded
to don the robes of an ecclesiastical dignitary let his hair
shirt stick out at the neck. Dedicated to our Lady of
Poverty, yet as Chancellor of Castille he used the revenues of the realm to convert, cow, or expel the Moors.
Monastic immorality and clerical concubinage were rigorously banned. A crusader, he organized and harangued
the troops which crossed the straits to attack the infidels
in Africa. All of these roles, though incongruous, epi-
tomized the many aspects of the Church of the Middle
Ages. But the Cardinal was also the founder of the University of Alcalá with chairs in medicine, anatomy, and
Hebrew, and it was he who engineered the publication
of the entire Bible in the original tongue, called the
Complutensian Polyglot in 1522. Erasmus anticipated
him only on the New Testament in 1516. Here was the
Church allied with the Renaissance.

Following Ximenes in the late fifteenth and early sixteenth century, Spain enjoyed a liberal interlude when
the influence of Erasmus was prevalent. Catholicism in
general throughout Europe became more latitudinarian
since there was no longer any great menace from the
effete medieval sects, nor from the nominal converts
from Judaism and Islam in Spain, nor were there any
major wars in the first two decades of the century. In
this brief period flourished a movement ill defined yet
definitely discernible and now sometimes comprised under the word *evangelism*. One ought to add, perhaps,
*Catholic* evangelism because Protestants were called
evangelical and, to this day in Europe, are commonly
referred to as *Evangéliques, Evangelici, Evangelische.*

This Catholic movement had a strongly mystical and ethical tone with a devotion to Christian scholarship. Erasmus was its most international representative. In France among the leaders were Lefèvre d'Etaples, Bishop Briçonnet and his circle at Meaux, and the sister of King Francis, Marguerite of Navarre. In Italy there were several foci. One was at Naples, at that time a Spanish dependency. Here a Spaniard, Juan Valdes, gathered at his retreat on the Island of Ischia men and women of the Italian aristocracy to engage in spiritual conversations. His meditations for such occasions are recorded in his *One Hundred and Ten Divine Considerations*. His mysticism is reminiscent of Tauler, and his decrying of externalism in the matter of pilgrimages, fasts, and celibacy recalls the inward piety of Erasmus and the Brethren of the Common Life. Another circle centered on Rome and was called the *Oratory of Divine Love,* a company of some fifty laymen and high ecclesiastics dedicated to the reform of the Church and particularly insistent that bishops should attend to their flocks. From this group emanated the memorandum on the reform of the Church addressed to Pope Paul III. (*See Reading 8, No. I.*)

Already two types of reform began to emerge within Catholicism. There was one which insisted on morals but was very indifferent or broad as to doctrine. The leader of this party was Cardinal Contarini who was very hopeful of reunion with the Protestants because he was ready to concede justification by faith. The other party was rigid alike as to deportment and doctrine and would stamp out dereliction both in deed and in creed. The leader of this group was Cardinal Caraffa, later Pope Paul IV. As the tension with the Protestants grew more acute, Caraffa was to gain the ascendancy. In 1542 when Contarini failed in his reunion plan with the Protestants, Caraffa secured the institution of the Roman Inquisition with himself named as one of the chief inquisitors. (*See Reading 8, No. III.*) Then the liberal reformers divided into three groups. There were those who stayed within the Catholic Church, remained in Italy and solaced themselves with mystical piety, making cloisters of their own hearts. Such was the course taken by Valdes and some of his disciples. Even so he would hardly have been spared investigation had he not died early. Others, more

pronounced in their criticism of Rome, stayed in Italy
and went to the stake, like the papal secretary Carne-
secchi. Some who never thought of themselves at all as
rebels, yet because of their association with liberals were
suspect, also were incarcerated. Cardinal Morone, for
example, passed the Pontificate of Paul IV in the prison
of the Inquisition. A third group went into exile. These
Italian refugees had difficulty in adjusting themselves to
the forms of Protestantism already encrusted. They had
not fled the rigidities of Rome to put their necks under a
more stringent yoke. The northern reformers found the
Italians restive, inquisitive, and disturbing. Some of them
became Anabaptists and some Anti-trinitarians, though
some made a successful adjustment, especially to Calvinism. The one movement which took on shape among
these exiles was the Socinian, named for Fausto Sozzini,
with its strength mainly in Poland where some of the
old feudal nobility became converts. In this instance
doctrinal Anti-trinitarianism and the social program of
Anabaptism were combined.

The Jesuits. The Catholic Reformation headed by
Caraffa (Paul IV) was dedicated to more than repres-
sion. New orders were founded to implement the program. The Theatines, founded in part by Caraffa, were
parish priests bound by monastic vows and dedicated to
the cure of souls. The Capuchins were a new branch of
the spiritual Franciscans seeking to revive the fervor, the
simplicity and poverty of the radical tradition. Chary at
first of learning they became great evangelistic preachers.
The most significant and important of the orders of the
Catholic Reformation was the Jesuit, founded by Ignatius
Loyola, a Spanish nobleman who, disqualified for military exploits by a shattered leg, committed himself to the
militia of Jesus under the ensign of Our Lady. Although
a grown man he set himself to go to school with boys.
The learning which the erudite Capuchins renounced,
he sought to acquire because apparently he already per-
ceived that the Protestant menace could not be overcome
simply by inquisitorial fires. For himself he was repeatedly investigated by the Inquisition because he had the
temerity without ecclesiastical authorization to commence reform at the bottom with fellow students and
their prostitutes. The Church, he recognized, was not to

be cleansed by memoranda presented to the Pope by
committees of the Cardinals, but rather by an irrepressible student, who, if he had been stopped, might easily
have become a rebel. One has the feeling repeatedly that
the line between the Protestant rebels and the Catholic
reformers was very tenuous. Matteo Basso, the founder
of the Capuchins, was another of those incorrigibles,
who presumably would have gone his own way if the
Church had not approved. Whether or not these horsemen
of the Lord should pull with or against the chariot of
the Church was a decision resting with the administra-
tors. As in an earlier period Waldo became a heretic
and Francis a saint, because the one was rejected and
the other approved, so in the sixteenth century Loyola
might have become a schismatic and Luther a saint had
the Popes reversed their treatment.

But, of course, this is all conjecture. Loyola did believe in military obedience to God and to the Pope. His
*Spiritual Exercises* contained a prayer to God which is
as completely submissive as anything in John Calvin.
"Take, O Lord, and receive all my liberty, my memory,
my understanding, and all my will, all I have and possess.
You have given it to me. To You, Lord, I return it. All
is Yours. Dispose of it entirely according to Your will.
Give me Your love and grace because that is enough for
me."

Calvin and Loyola ought to have been able to understand each other. But there was this tremendous difference, that to religious obedience Loyola added ecclesiastical obedience to the Pope and, under the Pope, to
the general of the order. Not for the Jesuit to reason
why. He should accept any assignment whether to the
faithful, the heretic, or the infidel and in any part of the
globe. (*See Reading 8, No. II.*)

The Jesuits undertook to recall the errant, to entice the
diffident, and to allure the alien. Their object was to
induce non-practicing Catholics to avail themselves of
the saving sacraments of the Church and, to this end,
the way should be made as easy as possible. This does
not mean that the end justifies the means. This phrase is
nowhere discoverable in Jesuit literature. Rather the
order endorsed the principle of *probabilism*, which means
that wherever legitimately a doubt may be entertained

as to guilt, the sinner is to be given the benefit. The quality of sin depends on the intention. Since intentions are very difficult to assess, the more charitable interpretation should be deemed probable and the penitent absolved on this assumption.

The relaxation of rigor in the confessional, however, was not the primary way to win souls. They must be instructed. The Jesuits committed themselves to the task of education. Their schools rival the Calvinist academies. Significantly, in the United States most of our colleges on the Atlantic seaboard, practically all in New England, and many in the Middle and Far West are Calvinist foundations established by Congregationalists or Presbyterians. In the Catholic world many great institutions of learning in this country are manned by the Jesuits. One thinks of the universities of Georgetown and Fordham.

Another great work of the Jesuits was foreign missions. In this they were not alone. The other outstanding order was the Franciscan. There was a geographical division of labor. The Jesuits were active around the region of the Great Lakes in North America and, in South America, in Peru. The very name Des Moines means in French "the monks." The Franciscans operated in Mexico, Florida, and southern California—witness the name San Francisco. There is one curious point here, namely, that the Jesuits who originated in Spain were French in the New World, and the Franciscans who began in Italy were Spanish. But this only illustrates the international character of the Catholic monastic orders and, for that matter, of the Church itself.

Protestantism in the same period was not active in foreign missions. The reason was, in part, that energy was wholly consumed in the endeavor to win converts from Catholicism. The emissaries sent out from Geneva, carrying on often a clandestine mission in France, were as intrepid as any of the Jesuits among the Iroquois. Unfortunately, the Calvinists were not sufficient to undertake also the conversion of the Indians, though after the colonization of New England in the following century Indian missions were then established. Even the Anabaptists, who laid a missionary obligation upon every member, directed their labors primarily to winning adherents from other Christian bodies. Protestant foreign missions did not flourish until the time of the evangelical revivals of the eighteenth century.

**The Council of Trent.**     Another work of the Catholic Reformation was the clarification and modification of Catholic dogma at the Council of Trent. This is such a landmark that historians speak of Tridentine and pre- and post-Tridentine Catholicism. It was here that Thomism became ascendant. (*See Reading 9, No. III.*)

The summoning of a council had long been resisted by the Popes because of the fear of resurgent conciliarism which might well destroy that centralization of the Church's organization, so imperative in dealing with the centralized national states. There was reason for fear because conciliarism as an ideal was not extinct, certainly not in France where the Sorbonne had issued an appeal to a general council shortly before Luther's appeal. In fact, Luther had modeled his upon it. And if conciliarism came into vogue, the papacy would be reduced to a constitutional monarchy. Civil rulers urged a council to deal with all of the disorders within and without the Church. The Popes stalled. The last council had been the Fifth Lateran terminating in 1518. Another was not summoned until the Council of Ratisbonne in 1541, if it can indeed be called a council. It was a gathering of some Catholics and Protestants in an abortive effort at understanding. In the interval, ecclesiastical matters had been discussed and settled at Diets of the German Empire, which were secular assemblies, to the great distaste of the Pope. If this were not to go on, the alternative was a council under ecclesiastical auspices. The increasing disruption of Europe made it imperative. Germany was split. England and Scandinavia had seceded. Despite the risks a council must be summoned, and a council was called at Trent in the year 1545 and continued at intervals in session until 1563.

**The Augsburg Confession.**     The main task confronting the body was the refutation of error and the clarification of truth. The Council could scarcely avoid casting many of its pronouncements into a Protestant mold in order to expose the heresies of the adversary. Before the Council lay the Augsburg Confession of 1530. It was an irenic document composed with the hope that the emperor, because of it, might accord toleration to the Lutherans. It was divided into two parts. (*See Reading 9, No. I.*) The first consisted of positive affirmations; the second of a refutation of popish errors. Yet many points are repudiated by inference rather than expressly. The sacraments are not flatly declared to be only two, though none are enumerated save baptism and the Lord's Supper, and the Church is declared to be wherever these were administered. The doctrine of transubstantiation is not rejected with the use of this term, but the Lord's body and blood are said to be truly present under the form of bread and wine "and any opposite doctrine is to be rejected." Even the sacrifice of the Mass is repudiated only by implication, when it is said that Christ made the one oblation by His passion. The doctrine of justification by faith is, of course, stressed and is declared to be of unspeakable comfort. Since the Lutherans were accused of ethical indifference and of making man into an inert log incapable of good, stress is placed on man's ability to fulfill all of the civil virtues and on his duty to perform good works not with an eye to reward which he can never merit but out of gratitude and obedience to God. Monasticism, as a way of gaining merit before God, is reproved, and the invocation of the saints declared to be unscriptural. One might have thought that these last points would more appropriately have been transferred to the next section, namely, on the abuses of Rome in need of correction. This section includes the withdrawal of the cup from the laity, the saying of the Mass for money, the treatment of the Mass as itself a good work, and private Masses said for the dead by the priest alone with no one else communing. The enumeration of all sins in confession is declared to be unnecessary and impossible. Distinction of meats and days is condemned as a new legalism. Monastic vows should not be taken. If they are so binding, why have they been dispensed on occasion by the Popes? The exaltation of celibacy is deprecated. The power of the keys is simply the power to preach the Word, to pardon or condemn sin, and to administer the sacraments. The Church should not impede government. The Gospel is to be interpreted according to its own

intent. The changes here proposed, concludes the Confession, need not disrupt the unity of the Church. Many
minor matters have not been mentioned, among them
indulgences. So far had the initial controversy receded.
One observes no clear statement here as to where authority lies. The Scriptures are to be interpreted according to their intent. Does this mean that each may make
his own interpretation?

**The Thirty-nine Articles.** Before the Council of
Trent terminated its sessions, the Anglican Thirty-nine
Articles were also available. (*See Reading 9, No. II.*)
They did not differ markedly from the Augsburg Confession and for good reason. In 1555 the emperor had
granted toleration to the Lutherans in restricted areas on
the basis of the Augsburg Confession. If, then, the English settlement did not exceed in doctrinal radicalism
the German, Elizabeth had a point of vantage in dealing with the continental Catholic powers. The Thirty-
nine Articles are at one with the Augsburg Confession
as to justification by faith and the need for good works
proceeding from faith. The Church, here as there, is
where the Word is preached and the sacraments administered. But the sacraments are declared expressly to
be only two, and transubstantiation is named in order
to be rejected. Monastic vows, clerical marriage, distinc-
tions of meats and days receive similar treatment. There
is a Calvinist tinge in that it is not justification but predestination which is declared to be an unspeakable comfort, and on the Lord's Supper there is a Calvinist flavor
where it is said that "the body of Christe is geuen,
taken and eaten in the Supper only after an heuenly
and spirituall manner." On the question of authority
there is less ambiguity. The books of the Old Testament
and of the New Testament are listed with the omission
of the Old Testament Apocrypha as authority to "establish any doctrene." Elizabeth inserted in Article Twenty
that the Church "hath auchthoritie in controuersies of
fayth." Yet the same article avers that the Church though
"a keper of holy writ ought not to decree anything
agaynst the same." The next article says that "Generall
Counsels may err." Who then interprets Scripture? The
articles of the Church, over which the queen was the

"Supreme Governor," point out that councils may be called only by the "commaundements and wyll of princes" and, of course, civil magistrates receive their due, though it is expressly noted that "we geve not to our princes the ministering either of God's Word or of the Sacraments."

The Council of Trent left no ambiguity. The authoritative Scriptures are the New Testament and the Old Testament including its Apocrypha. The authoritative version is the Latin Vulgate. Holy Mother Church is to judge of its interpretation. The decrees roundly affirm that there are seven sacraments. They can be performed not by all Christians but only by those ordained and the ordination is indelible for life. The priesthood of all believers is entirely rejected. The sacraments contain grace. They have an efficacy of their own beyond the faith of the recipient. Transubstantiation is expressly affirmed, and the Mass is a sacrifice. (*See Reading 9, No. III.*)

Naturally the discussion of justification by faith is quite long, and verbally Trent might appear to be in agreement with Augsburg, but the explications make this quite impossible. Trent affirms that man is indeed saved only by the grace of God, but this operates at two levels. The prevenient grace conferred in baptism enables a man to cooperate with God and this cooperation merits reward. Faith itself must be conjoined with hope and charity. All three lie in the power of man to give or to withhold. Therefore, to have faith becomes of itself a deed performed by man entitling him to credit. This is to make of faith precisely what Luther called a good work. The ultimate difference between Catholicism and Protestantism in the sixteenth century is that, according to the latter, man can do absolutely nothing to acquire a claim on God, whereas the Catholic maintains that man can do something by reason of which God will treat him differently than if he had not done it. The notion of reward and penalty is not excluded. This is still more plain when penance is called a second plank after the shipwreck of grace is lost. And this also is why justification can be increased by advancing from virtue to virtue. Luther could never accord such recognition to the works of man. Trent had vindicated Erasmus, who in his first

controversy with Luther had said that the basic difference was this—that Luther ascribed absolutely everything to God and absolutely nothing to man in the
process of salvation.

## — 7 —

# PERSECUTION, REBELLION, WAR, AND LIBERTY

**Persecution.** The confessional differences of the
sixteenth century were more than once dealt with by
disputations and councils, but when reason failed force
was invoked. All the major parties believed in the pro-
priety of constraint. In their eyes heresy would damn
souls to eternal fires and bring the divine displeasure
upon the earthly community. No crime could be greater
than that which destroys immortal souls rather than
ephemeral bodies, which counterfeits divine truth, com-
mits *lèse majesté* against the Sovereign of the universe
and treason to the kingdom of heaven. All of the penalties which apply to such offenses when committed against
earthly majesty are doubly fitting when heavenly majesty
is offended. Besides, the tranquillity of kingdoms depends
upon the support of religion and religion itself must least
of all be divided. The common assumption was that two
religions could not exist peaceably side by side in the
same place. For that reason efforts were made, when
persuasion failed, to extirpate the direst of all foes to the
body politic.

The Catholics had recourse to the stake, and many
institutions were alerted to help. In France the municipal
authorities might act, as might the *Parlements* (not Par-

liaments but courts). One of the most notorious in this regard was the *Parlement de Paris*. In addition there was the Inquisition. We have observed the establishment of the Roman Inquisition in 1542. Some of the cities like Naples and Venice were very obstructionist with regard to its operation, but as the century advanced the opposition diminished.

A striking example of persecution in France is afforded by an incident in the reign of Francis I. (*See Reading 12, No. I.*) The king, desirous of forfending divine anger incurred by the public posting on the part of Protestants of "Placards" in France, instituted a procession in which all of the pomp of medieval pageantry was displayed. In contrast to the bedecked dignitaries of Church and State the king walked as a penitent with a lighted taper. When all due reverence had been shown to the priceless relics of the saints and the body of the Lord, the king and his entourage had dinner with the Bishop of Paris and topped off the meal by watching the burning of Protestant heretics. Protestants, in their turn, did not burn Catholics, for they believed that the core of the two faiths was residual in the Church, but they did burn and drown heretics to the left of themselves. The Anabaptists, as we have seen, were killed by the Catholics with fire and by the Protestants with water. The Anti-trinitarian and Anabaptist, Michael Servetus, had the singular fate to be burned in effigy in France by the Catholics and in actuality by the Protestants in Geneva. (*See Reading 12, No. II.*)

**Rebellion.** In all of these instances persecution was directed only against individuals, but soon groups came to be involved. Military alliances were formed and wars of religion ensued. In many instances they involved revolt against the constituted authorities, and then a very trying dilemma of conscience was presented. All parties agreed that the State is ordained of God. Luther had been very insistent that the subject is to suffer tyranny rather than to rebel, but if the ruler persecutes the true religion, what then? Is one merely to suffer or may the godless tyrant be resisted? Luther had held that the Gospel is not to be defended by force of arms. The problem became more acute after his death in Germany when Charles V, after twenty-five years of involvement with rivals, found himself at last free to intervene and enforce a religious settlement to the great disadvantage of the Protestants. He offered them a compromise in the form of the so-called Augsburg Interim to be valid in the interim up to the meeting of a general council. It conceded so little that the great majority of the Protestants would not touch it, and as already noted, many went into exile in England. In 1550 when Charles was prepared to employ Spanish troops for the enforcement of his plan, the Protestants of Magdeburg grappled with the right of revolution in the name of religion. Their conclusion was that, although a private citizen is not to rebel, an inferior magistrate, being ordained of God, may resist a superior magistrate. A theory of constitutionalism underlies this contention. The higher rulers are bound by their oath to the constitution, particularly in the case of the Holy Roman Empire, and above all to the truth of God. If then they are recreant, they may be resisted even unto blood. (*See Reading 11, No. I.*)

Speedily, as already observed, the situation altered in England, and in 1553 the Catholic Mary succeeded the Protestant Edward. Then the English Protestants canvassed the right of revolution, and Bishop Ponet (*see Reading 11, No. II*) again invoked the inferior magistrate against the higher. Christopher Goodman (*see Reading 11, No. III*) was more radical, holding that if the magistrate violates the truth of God, he is no longer a magistrate, and in an emergency may be resisted by the sword of any citizen. John Knox's word to Mary was in the same vein. (*See Reading 11, No. IV.*) This theory opens the way for resistance by assassination, of which, before the century was out, there were to be a good many examples. In Geneva and France, Calvin had the same view of the legitimacy of resistance only under a *magistrat inférieur,* and for him this meant in France a prince of the blood. The real trouble with the conspiracy of Amboise, of which he unequivocally disapproved (*see Reading 6, No. VIc*), was that it had been engineered under the wrong auspices, and when later the sword was raised by the Prince Condé of the House of Bourbon, Calvin did not demur. During the course of the wars in France, more and more radical political theory was elaborated. The peak is found in the anony-

mous *Vindiciae contra tyrannos* (*see Reading 11, No. V*)
where a contract theory of government is espoused. The
work had less influence in France at the time than
subsequently.

Practice was not behind theory. The first Duke of
Guise, Henry by name, was assassinated by a Protestant.
The Catholics retaliated. The attempt on the life of
Coligny, the ensuing massacre of Saint Bartholomew, the
assassination of Henry III, and later of Henry IV and
William of Orange, emanated from Catholic quarters, not
to forget the plots on the life of Elizabeth. And such
assassinations of individuals were dwarfed by massacres
of thousands and wars decimating France and the Low
Countries.

**Edicts and Wars.** A brief survey of the edicts and
so-called settlements of the religious issue throughout the
century will serve to outline the tortuous course leading
to eventual resolution. In 1521 came the ban against
Martin Luther whereby he was to be delivered up undoubtedly for burning at the stake. (*See Reading 10,
No. I.*) But he was spirited away, as we have seen, and
when he reemerged the Catholic powers were not too
blind to perceive that he had become a force for order
against the more chaotic tendencies among his followers.
Besides, he had powerful support. Therefore, the Diet of
Nürnberg decreed in 1524 (*see Reading 10, No. II*) that
the Edict of Worms should be enforced "insofar as
might be possible." Lutheranism made in consequence
such gains that the Diet of Speier of 1526 left each ruler
free to act as he would answer to God and the emperor.
(*See Reading 10, No. III.*) By 1529 the situation had
altered. An attempt at an alliance between the Swiss and
the German Protestants at Marburg in the spring of that
year had failed. Surprisingly large agreement had been
attained, but on the question of the Lord's Supper dis-
agreement remained, and in any case Luther disapproved
of military measures. Hence at Speier in 1529 the majority rescinded the unanimous decision of the previous
Diet and decreed that Lutheranism might be tolerated
in those territories where it could not be suppressed
without danger to the civil peace, but Catholic minorities
must be allowed; whereas in Catholic territory, Protestant minorities would not be suffered. Against this in-

vidious arrangement the Protestant minority protested, and thereby acquired the name *Protestant*. Be it observed, however, that what was said was this: "We protest and testify," and there was greater concern to testify than to protest. (*See Reading 10, No. IV.*)

The Diet of Augsburg in 1530 refused recognition to the Augsburg Confession of that year and gave the Protestants until the fifteenth of April of the year following in which to make their submission. The threat of war was implicit. In the meantime in Switzerland religious war had broken out between Zürich and the Catholic cantons. In the second Cappell war Zwingli himself was killed carrying sword and helmet, a minister on the field of battle, a relic of the crusading idea. Luther highly discountenanced such a mingling of the offices of the minister and the warrior. The second peace of Cappell in 1531 was the first legal recognition of the principle of territorial division according to religion. Zwinglianism was to be recognized in the canton of Zürich and Catholicism in the neighboring canton. Each should refrain from molesting the other. (*See Reading 10, No. VI.*)

When the fifteenth of April arrived in 1531, the emperor was not in a position to apply the constraint contemplated. Consequently, the peace of Nürnberg in 1532 bound both sides to keep the peace until the meeting of a general council. (*See Reading 10, No. VII.*)

A lull occurred on the continent during which time England joined the dissidents. Hostilities were resumed in Germany, as already noted, when Charles tried to enforce the Augsburg Interim and the Lutherans at Magdeburg endorsed armed resistance. The Schmalkald War followed. Charles was eventually expelled from Germany, and the outcome was the Peace of Augsburg in 1555. (*See Reading 10, No. VIII.*) This definitely established on a wide scale the territorial principle that each ruler should be responsible for the form of religion in his area. Here is the principle of *cuius regio eius religio*, "whose region his religion." This Latin phrase nowhere occurs in the peace, which is entirely in German, nor is there any equivalent. The original of the formula cannot be definitely determined, but at any rate it is not discoverable in the sixteenth century. Yet the

idea is much older. In the Middle Ages many churches
had been founded by patrons who assumed a responsibility for the ministerial incumbent. The free imperial
cities considered themselves answerable for the conduct
of monks, nuns, and the demeanor of the clergy within
their precincts. The application of this principle provided
legal justification for the ecclesiastical partition of Germany. Lutheranism was to be allowed in those places
where it was in the ascendant at the time of the Treaty
of Passau in 1552. The problem of minorities should be
solved by an exchange of populations, who should be un-
impeded in the sale of their goods and in the transfer.
This was called the *ius emigrandi* and enshrined liberty
of a sort. But if any higher ecclesiastic became a Protestant, his goods and revenues were to remain with the
Church. The failure to observe this proviso was one of
the reasons for the Thirty Years' War in the next century. Other varieties of Protestantism such as Anabaptism, Zwinglianism, and Calvinism were not recognized,
and the subsequent invasion of Germany by Calvinism
was another reason for the later conflict. When Lutheranism had thus attained recognition, revolutionary concepts were dropped, and Lutheranism eventually so far
succumbed to a supine endorsement of the State that the
earlier intransigence was almost completely forgotten.

Calvinism was to be the great exponent of rebellion
and war. This was true in France, Holland, Scotland,
and England. In France the fight was greatly compli-
cated because it became fused with a struggle between
the crown and the nobility for exclusive control. Several
of the great families became identified with religious
parties. The most fanatically Catholic house was that of
Guise. We have already noted as members of this house
Mary, the Queen Regent of Scotland; the mother of
Mary Queen of Scots; and Mary's brothers, Duke Henry
of Guise and the Cardinal of Lorraine. It was Duke
Francis who precipitated the wars of religion by firing
upon Protestants engaged in worship. The most con-
sistently Protestant house was that of Chatillon whose
most distinguished representative was the Admiral Coligny. Then there were two houses which successively
ruled in France, the house of Valois and the house of
Bourbon. Both were concerned for the tranquillity of

the land and the continuance of its dynasty even more
than for religious uniformity. The Bourbons, while out
of power were mainly Protestant and some were so by
conviction, like the Queen of Navarre and her husband's
brother, the Prince of Condé; but her husband, Anthony,
was vacillating and so also her son, later to be Henry
IV of France. Among the Valois the most influential was
not a Valois but the Italian, Catherine de' Medici, the
wife and later the widow of Henry II and the mother
of Francis II, Charles IX, and Henry III among others.
She desired to pacify France by a compromise in religion. Both the Valois and the Bourbons belonged in-
cipiently to the party which came later to be called the
*Politiques,* which placed the political interest above the
religious.

Catherine succeeded in 1559 in summoning a colloquy
of Catholics and Protestants at Poissy where indeed
agreement was not reached. Yet the result was the Edict
of January of 1560 which granted tolerance to the
Huguenots in limited areas. When Duke Henry of Guise
thereafter found them worshipping, as he believed outside of the permitted enclosure, he attacked at Vassy
(1562). This massacre set off three wars lasting ten
years, and all of them were inconclusive. Catherine made
another attempt at Compromise in 1572, symbolized by
a marriage between a Catholic Valois princess and the
Protestant, Henry of Navarre of the house of Bourbon.
The plan was wrecked by the attempt on the life of
Coligny instituted by Duke Francis, the son of the murdered Duke Henry of Guise, on the assumption that
Coligny was privy to the plot on his father's life. The
failure to kill the Protestant chief with a single shot led
to his murder along with that of his followers in the
massacre of St. Bartholomew in the month of August,
1572. The result was another series of wars punctuated
by assassinations. The upshot of it all was that Henry of
Navarre emerged as the heir to the throne, which, however, he found himself unable to occupy because he was
a Protestant. At last he decided to pacify the kingdom by
changing his religion.

**Settlements and Liberty.** Then came the problem
of the religious settlement. The principle of territorialism was already well recognized. Switzerland was di-

vided. Germany was divided. The Low Countries likewise were divided between Holland and Belgium. Yet
such a dismemberment of France was a grievous con-
templation, and the king was so imbued with the ideal of
a unified, centralized, monarchical nation that he could
not consent to such a solution. A new plan had been
introduced briefly in Poland. It was called the *Pax Dissi-
dentium* (*see Reading 10, No. IX*), meaning the peace
of those who agree to differ. It was only among varieties
of Protestants, however. The Calvinists, the Lutherans,
and the Hussites agreed to accord each other mutual
recognition and without assignment to any particular
areas. The arrangement was short-lived, and since the
Catholics were not parties to the peace, the plan without
modification could not be transferred to France. Elizabeth in England had succeeded by a policy of comprehension which aimed at one religion for the whole country with minimal demands and ambiguous formulation.
Yet this scheme applied only to the Protestants. Henry
had a more difficult problem. The two groups most
opposed to each other were both intransigent and France
should not be divided. The Edict of Nantes was something of a combination of territorialism and mutual recognition. (*See Reading 10, No. X.*) Since the Huguenots
were to be eligible to all public offices, this meant that
in the councils of state the representatives of the two
religions would be at each other's side, but when it came
to worship there was still a localization. The Huguenots
were to be free to exercise their religion fully only in
those cities which they had held in a military sense at
the close of the wars. These cities as a guarantee were
to be garrisoned with Huguenot troops at State expense,
but only for the space of eight years. Henry did not relish
this embryonic state within the State, and in the end the
logic of *un roi, une loi, une foi,* "one king, one law, one
faith," was to lead to the Revocation of the Edict of
Nantes, when in 1685 absolutism triumphed under Louis
XIV.

The attainment of religious liberty had, nevertheless,
been advanced by these tentative solutions of the sixteenth century, and many ideas had been voiced which
subsequently issued in a complete liberty in religion.
The execution of Michael Servetus at Geneva in 1553

precipitated a sharp controversy among Protestants. The champion of liberty was Sebastian Castellio, at the time professor of Greek at the University of Basal. He had even earlier expressed objection to constraint in the dedication of his Bible to Edward VI. The contrast is marked with Calvin's letter to the young king's uncle, the Duke of Somerset. (*See Reading 6, No. VIA.*) Castellio in an anonymous work entitled *Concerning Heretics and Whether They Are to Be Coerced by the Sword of the Magistrate* (1554, *see Reading 12, No. IV*) in many respects shifted the emphasis in religion away from the points over which persecution was exercised. He did not deny the importance of dogma, but differentiated dogmas into the important and the indifferent, those necessary and those negligible *for salvation*. That was the point, not whether they were true but whether God would require a right judgment on these points if one were to be saved. Here was a distinction between the fundamentals and the nonessentials destined to a long history in the toleration controversy. Among the nonessentials Castellio listed predestination, the state of souls after death, whether the risen Christ is everywhere diffused, as the Lutherans claimed or localized at the right hand of the Father in heaven, as the Calvinists affirmed, and even the doctrine of the Trinity was considered nonessential. Dogma, as a whole, was disparaged in comparison with deportment. An upright man even though he be in error, said Castellio, will not be despised by the Lord. This assertion meant a shift from correctness to conviction as of prime importance in the eyes of God. The theologians of the Middle Ages had recognized that the erroneous conscience is binding, but not that it has any rights. These are enjoyed only by a right conscience. Most of the reformers agreed and complained of the persecution of their own party simply on the ground that they were right. But Castellio pointed out that Servetus might have been saved had he been willing to recant and deny his convictions. Because he refused, because he told the truth in the sense of what he believed to be the truth, for this reason he was burned and had he recanted, his moral disintegration would have been far worse than any error to which he clung. This relativiz-

ing of conscience was not to become a widespread attitude until the following century.

The doctrine of predestination was turned against the
persecutors. If eternal salvation is already predetermined,
how can persecution alter the outcome? The predesti-
narians could reply only that it cannot and that the
purpose of persecution then, after all, is not to save
souls but rather to vindicate the honor of God. To
which came the reply: "Why cannot God take care of
Himself?"

An intellectual determinism was invoked by the liberals
who often did not believe in predestination as to salvation, but they did see that a man at a given moment
cannot believe what he does not believe any more than
he can see what he does not see. If he is to be brought
to sight his eyes must first be opened, and if he is to be
brought to believe his heart must be warmed and persuaded. Of the highest importance then is the development of the technique of persuasion. It certainly does
not include the use of the sword. It does require a renunciation of acrimony, bitterness and railing and a
desire for victory rather than for verity. Again stress was
laid on the inwardness of religion which cannot be con-
strained or created by the sword of the magistrate. (*See
Reading 12, No. IV.*)

These many religious considerations were further rein-
forced in the political and economic spheres. William of
Orange observed that his country was the mart of
Christendom and would lose her preeminence if con-
vulsed from within and impeded from without in the
exercise of trade on account of religion. The political
considerations have already been mentioned, particularly
in France where the dissevering of the kingdom appeared a greater evil than the toleration of two religions
within the confines of a single state. There were also
increasingly rational considerations which sometimes
raised a doubt only with regard to the most controverted
points and were insistent that they must be doubtful
because they were controverted. Sometimes, however,
more drastic criticism impugned the truth even of Christian fundamentals. But of this we find almost nothing in
the sixteenth century.

— 8 —

# THE EFFECTS OF THE REFORMATION

**The Disruption of Christendom.** When one comes
to assess the effects of the Reformation on subsequent
history the most indisputable consequence is the definitive
disruption of Christendom. The medieval sects had
weakened the structure during the course of the previous
three hundred years, but their force was largely spent.
The rupture of the sixteenth century was widespread
and lasting. All Christians deplore this division and
each party blames the other. The Catholics upbraid the
Protestants with a refusal to submit to divinely instituted
authority. The Protestants blame the Catholics for de-
clining to endorse the truth of God. Some today chide
them both for their obduracy and wish that the middle
party of *Evangelism,* the school of Erasmus, might have
triumphed with its comparative indifference and lati-
tudinarianism as to dogma and its insistence on upright-
ness but not asceticism in conduct. Since this moderate
reform did not succeed no one can tell whether it might
have done so. Erasmus himself, at times, doubted whether
his deft tappings could effect a dent.

But be that as it may, the great rift is not to be counted
wholly on the side of debit. There are different levels
of unity and a breach in the external structure is entirely compatible with a renewal of the spirit. The
Church of the Renaissance was externally united, but
lax, loose, frequently frivolous, and tinctured with secularism. The Reformation quickened again the religious
life of Europe and gave new vitality to the Christian
consciousness.

Nor is the cleavage absolute. Movements toward
Church unity between Catholics and Protestants have
proved indeed to be abortive, but mutual respect has
increased, and notably during World War II when, association in the underground caused both to see that
their differences were trivial when set over against the

ravages of a rampant secularism. Protestantism has exhibited both divisive and unitive tendencies. Even little sects have ramified into spreading trees. On the other hand, many branches have come together. The Augsburg Confession was itself a triumph for the spirit of unity because it was but a single Lutheran confession rather than four, and the Wittenberg Concord of 1536 brought together the Lutherans and the Swiss. Cranmer endeavored to bring to pass an Ecumenical Protestant Conference in England.

**Teaching and Life.** If one inquires as to the positive and intentional effects of the Reformation, then one should look at the teaching and the life. Each side professed to have purified the teaching. As for the life, the Catholic Reformation did correct the prevalent financial extortion, the trafficking in holy things, and the flagrant sexual immorality of the clergy and the monks. As for Protestantism, one has to distinguish varieties. The Anabaptists set for themselves an extremely rigorous mode of behavior which very properly has been called "an inner worldly asceticism," that is to say, a spirit of rigor and renunciation practiced within the framework of political, economic, and family institutions. Anabaptism, however, did not stay entirely within the framework and particularly withdrew from politics. Calvinism, likewise, was rigoristic but more disposed to participate in the common life. Lutheranism was accused, by the other varieties, of indifference to morals, on the ground that we were saved by faith and not by works. This charge the Lutheran stoutly repudiated, and as a matter of fact, statistical studies of German towns demonstrate in Lutheran areas a very great improvement in sexual morality as a consequence of the Reformation.

The most notable difference between the confessions in the ethical sphere was the abolition of monasticism, which meant that a segregated area in which to practice a higher morality was gone and the more rigorous precepts of the Gospel must be exemplified in the midst of the common life, but this does not mean that the spirit of monasticism was extinct. Its rigorism survived chiefly in the form of heroism, rather than of asceticism. The distinction is that heroism renounces something deemed good in itself, whereas asceticism eschews that which is branded as evil. Albert Schweitzer was heroic, not ascetic, when he first went out to Africa as a doctor and left behind his beloved organ, since there was no instrument capable of withstanding the ravages of tropical insects. When later, friends constructed an instrument entirely of metal and shipped it out to him, he exclaimed: "I feel like Abraham receiving back Isaac."

Catholicism, of course, retained monasticism but not without modifications. An outsider has the feeling that monasticism since the Reformation has been more activist than during the Middle Ages. The difference, of course, is not to be exaggerated because the medieval monasteries performed an important social role, and today the comtemplative forms of monasticism are enjoying a resurgence, particularly in the United States since the Second World War. Yet for the most part the new Catholic orders have been instituted to meet particular needs, such as foreign missions, school teaching, hospital care, or what not. Even cloistered nuns are not wholly remote from the concerns of the world.

Yet ethics was not the primary concern of the first Protestant reformers. This Luther distinctly said. We must therefore explore what the Reformation did for religion. The answers here are not simple because no subject is more elusive, but surely one is safe in saying that the Reformation induced a deeper inwardness in the religious life. By Luther, the individual was made to stand in naked confrontation with his God, his Redeemer, and his Judge. He became more important because he must live for himself, die for himself, and be saved for himself. Yet he was made so aware of his own creatureliness and impurity that all of his own worth and claims were cancelled and his complete reliance was upon his Maker and Master, through the inner experience of faith. Catholic piety was likewise affected. The trafficking in indulgences, the crass, magical view of the Mass, the mechanical operation of penance, all bargaining with God and even the desire to bet on the best chance of salvation—these all are gone in a hymn attributed to Saint Francis Xavier, and if the ascription be erroneous, at any rate the hymn emanates from the Spanish Catholicism of the sixteenth century. Although the stress is not on justification by faith one would feel

that Luther and Calvin could scarcely fail to cherish such
piety.

> My God, I love Thee;
>    Not because I hope for heaven thereby,
> Nor yet because who love Thee not
>    Must die eternally.
>
> Thou, O my Jesus,
>    Thou didst me upon the cross embrace;
> For me didst bear the nails and spear,
>    And manifold disgrace;
>
> Then why, O blessed Jesus Christ,
>    Should I not love Thee well?
> Not for the hope of winning heaven,
>    Or of escaping hell;
>
> Not with the hope of gaining aught
>    Not seeking a reward;
> But as Thyself hast loved me,
>    O ever-loving Lord!

**Social Effects.**   When one turns to the effects of the
Reformation in the social sphere, the study becomes
enormously complex because the Reformation, both
Catholic and Protestant, cannot be described in terms of
a simple unity and because the characteristically modern
ideas and institutions are themselves in need of reduc-
tion to their components. The Catholic Reformation
appears more unified than the Protestant but even here,
just as Imperial Rome was distributed over seven hills,
so ecclesiastical Rome presents no drab uniformity.
There are, in the Roman communion, liberals and con-
servatives, the uncouth and the refined, the authoritarian
and the latitudinarian, the active and the contemplative.
One marvels almost more at the diversity of Rome than
at the varieties of Protestantism. These, however, are
not to be denied, and four, or at least three, main types
must be taken into account—the Lutheran, the Reformed,
the Anabaptist, and sometimes the Anglican.

Let us pass, in brief review, some of the characteristic
modern attitudes and institutions, noting the bearing
upon them of the Reformation.

The first is nationalism. It may be cultural and it may
be political. Cultural nationalism is perhaps more congenial to Protestantism because Rome is so much more

nearly a universal church. On the other hand, the Church of Rome, fused with Irish nationalism and Protestantism, particularly in its Calvinist form, has been international. As for political nationalism the churches have sometimes been neutral, sometimes warm proponents, and sometimes critical, particularly in more recent times.

**Democracy.** Democracy is another concept with many ingredients. In the United States it is commonly assumed to include the doctrine of the limited sovereignty of the State, the rights of man, representative government, univeral franchise, the separation of Church and State, religious liberty, and the public schools.

With regard to the limited sovereignty of the State, the early reformers, Catholic and Protestant alike, insisted that the ruler is not God but is under God and therefore is not absolute. If the ruler goes counter to the true religion, he is disqualified as a ruler and may be deposed and perhaps even assassinated. But by the same token, if he is devoted to the service of the true religion, his position is then the more impregnable. Protestant theory could eventuate either in the divine right of kings in the case of James I or in the regicide practiced by Oliver Cromwell, and Catholic theory might abet revolution in Ireland or Poland and support absolutism in the case of Louis XIV of France.

With regard to the rights of man, this terminology does not come from the Reformation, but the idea was present. It was not, however, a creation of the Reformation, but a transmission from the Middle Ages of the great concept of natural law; that is to say, a universal morality recognizable by and binding upon all people everywhere. This was a legacy from classical antiquity fused by the Church with the Scriptures so that the law of nature was equated with the ethical precepts of the Ten Commandments. These certainly specify no rights of man, but they do enjoin upon all, kings included, not to murder, rob, lie, violate women, or bear false witness. This tradition of natural law has survived among the Western democracies, while it became extinguished in Fascist and Communist states. The Fascists avail themselves of the romantic view that morality is the product of an erratic vitality manifest now in one, now in another, people. Here is a secularized form of the doctrine

of predestination because the nation which is at the
moment endowed with this vitality is a chosen people
selected by nature to determine the course of the historical process. To that end it may make its own morality,
which the less endowed cannot be expected to understand,
but must accept. The ancient classical Christian tradition
of an inalienable core of duties and rights was further
elaborated in the Puritan Revolution and variously
equated with the liberties of the subject and the rights
of Englishmen. The overtone was Christian. In France,
liberty, equality and fraternity, though proclaimed in the
name of the Goddess of Reason, were nonetheless a
heritage from that Christian tradition which the Reformation transmitted.

Protestantism may well have contributed indirectly
to the concept of the rights of man because of the enhanced importance of the person, responsible for himself
before God. The conclusion was not drawn in the sixteenth century that the person therefore enjoyed the
right to follow an erroneous conviction. Yet the emphasis
on his duty to obey his own leading logically required
freedom to do so.

With regard to representative government neither
Catholicism nor Protestantism has been vastly concerned
as to the structure of the state. Catholicism appears to
affiliate most happily with governments highly centralized,
authoritarian like her own. Protestants have found those
forms congenial in which they were reared. Lutheranism
operated under the territorial German princes and Anglicanism under the Tudor monarchy, while Calvinism was
at home in the republicanism of the Swiss cities. Anabaptism fared best under kindly feudal lords, but even
they were regarded as of the world.

A distinction needs here to be drawn between endorsement, acquiescence, and opposition to political forms.
The churches have shown a capacity to come to terms
with varieties of governments which they do not prefer
because the primary demand is for a favorable attitude
toward the religion itself. For this reason Catholicism
gives the appearance of callous opportunism with regard
to democracy, monarchy, benevolent despotism, or even
military dictatorship. The Catholic Church has four
adamant requirements. Namely, that the government

must allow freedom to celebrate the sacraments, free
to hold property, freedom for the monastic orders, a⌐ ┘
freedom for Catholic education. Granted these four, then,
any government, presumably even a Communist, could
be tolerated and worked with. In practice, in Europe in
the modern era, the Catholic Church has supported in
France, Spain, and Austria the *anciens regimes,* in Italy
the local states in opposition to that unification which
would and did abrogate the estates of the Church; in
Poland revolutionary movements directed in the western
section again Protestant Prussia and in the eastern against
Orthodox Russia; in Belgium a republican movement
whose aim was separation from Holland; in Germany
opposition to everything Prussian because Prussia was
Protestant. In consequence the Center party, organized
by Catholics, became the exponent of liberalism. In the
United States, and only in the United States, did the
Catholic Church espouse democracy on the ground that
under the circumstances this form was the most advan-
tageous to the Church, at that time a small minority.
Now that Catholic strength has increased in the United
States these assertions are sometimes in a measure qualified.

The accommodation of Protestantism to various political forms has already been noted.

The extension of the franchise was not demanded by
any of the parties of the Reformation. It assumes intelli-
gence and political capacity on the part of the entire
populace. The Catholic Church has always held that
in matters of religion the laity should be instructed by
the clergy. Likewise in statecraft the common man is
not so well in a position to judge as is the ruler. This
view buttresses an authoritarian regime.

Protestantism no less in the beginning was authoritarian. For the authority of the Church was substituted
the authority of the Book with the assumption that its
meaning was perfectly obvious. Experience demonstrated
great diversity of opinion as to its meaning. Either, then,
one would have to reinstate an authoritarian human tribunal or else shift to a different view as to how truth is
obtained. The view came to prevail that truth emerges in
the course of a process in which individuals advance
hypotheses and are engaged in mutual criticism. Thus

in the clash of minds clarity emerges and a common view is achieved. This is precisely the democratic process. One might still claim that only the experts should be admitted to the debate, but experience has demonstrated in religion that, although indeed a technical question can be settled only by a specialist, nevertheless, spiritual insight may well be contributed by the illiterate.

The opportunity to test this method came in England in the Puritan Revolution when the spiritual successors of the Anabaptists, namely, the Independents, the Baptists, and the Quakers, in alliance sometimes with the Presbyterians clashed with the Anglicans and with the Stuart monarchy. In this whole ferment the radical sects participated. Imprisonment was now the only penalty rather than death, and even imprisonment proved to be a means of disseminating ideas. Under such circumstances the Quakers, who in many respects resemble the Anabaptists, did not withdraw from political life, except at the point of war, and their leader, William Penn, won a conspicuous and influential victory for the right of a jury to render an unintimidated verdict. Although none of these sects demanded a universal franchise because of the fear that the sinners might rule the saints, at the same time they gave the people of England a training in universal political participation. The demand for the universal franchise was, however, advanced by none of the Churches but rather by a political party called the Levelers, a group deeply imbued with Christian concepts. Their leader, John Lilburne, ended as a Quaker.

The separation of Church and State in the sixteenth century was demanded only by the Anabaptists. In the seventeenth century the Separatist churches of the Puritan Revolution, i.e., the Baptists, the Separatist Congregationalists, and the Quakers, revived the demand on the ground that the Church should comprise only the regenerate and the State should include the entire populace. In the American colonies the pattern was diverse. The Baptists in Rhode Island and the Quakers in Pennsylvania had no establishments, but the Congregationalists in New England, the Anglicans in Virginia, the Swedish Lutherans in Delaware, the Presbyterians in New York and New Jersey, all had State churches and the Catholics in Maryland might well have done so had they been free.

The reason for the ultimate separation was partly the triumph of Baptist ideas and partly the extreme pattern of diversity among churches which no longer made an exclusive claim to truth. If there were many religions and no one could be deemed uniquely true, then either all should be established or all disestablished, and the latter was the outcome. The Catholics, being at the time a small minority suffering under the establishment of Protestant Churches, welcomed the separation. Significantly, in the United States the separation of Church and State has been friendly. The government still favors religion and the churches pray for and seek to influence the government.

Be it observed that the separation of Church and State is not a necessary ingredient of democracy. Surely England is a democracy, but there the Anglican Church is established. Nor is the separation to be equated with religious liberty, which obtains in England despite the establishment.

When it comes to religious liberty, Protestantism has provided the primary area of debate. In Protestant lands liberty has made its most significant gains. But Catholicism is not required by its very nature to be persecuting and, in modern times, has abandoned the methods of the Inquisition. The grounds for liberty in Catholicism are fewer than in Protestantism. Persecution depends on three assumptions: (1) that one has the truth; (2) that this truth is supremely important; (3) that coercion will do some good. Protestantism can soften on all three counts since there is no absolute certainty as to truth, and the points over which persecution was formerly exercised are not now regarded as essential for salvation. In any case, coercion does not produce heartfelt conversion. Catholicism cannot compromise on the first two, but may concur with Protestants on the third.

On the matter of the schools, Catholicism and Protestantism alike are concerned that their children should receive religious instruction, but this cannot easily be given in the public schools in a land of diversified faiths. Hence, by law religion is not to be taught in the American public schools, though, as a matter of fact, a good deal is actually introduced, yet not enough to satisfy those with a deep religious concern. The Catholics are developing parochial schools. Some Protestants have done the same and may be driven more and more to this expedient, if secularism denudes public education of its religious core.

Economic Effects. The consequences of the Reformation in the economic sphere have been much debated. In particular, Calvinism has been credited with fostering the spirit of capitalism. A distinction must here be drawn between the structure of capitalism and the spirit of capitalism. The structure involving a moneyed economy, banking, bookkeeping, and credit, the charging of interest, all these had been highly developed in the period of the Renaissance and largely as a result of the international financial operations of the Papal State. The spirit of capitalism is one which directs man's endeavors to a furious pursuit of gain, not for the sake of gain, but because the endeavor itself ministers to God's glory. There are here several assumptions. The first is that man is called by God to work and to work hard in whatever calling he may be stationed. The secular occupations were rated higher in the eyes of God than the monastic life, so said Luther. Calvin is claimed in addition to have added that man can assure himself of his election by the fury of his labor, but not by the enjoyment of the fruits. He may gain, but he must not indulge. In that case he can do only two things with his money. He may give it away or turn it back into the business, thus accumulating a capital. In this way a morale is provided for unremitting toil alike on the part of the working classes, who are not to complain of their wages but glorify God by their work, and on the part of the entrepreneur, who is not to stop when he has made enough but carry on in stern discipline because this is the task to which he has been set. There is a further point that the Lord will prosper those whom he loveth. And finally there is no ban on the taking of interest.

By way of comment we may start with the last point. Calvin should not be held responsible for the removal of the ban on interest because both he and Luther retained the essence of the view of St. Thomas, who allowed a contract of mutual risk but not of fixed return. Profit, he said, may legitimately come to one who lends, provided he shares also in the loss. What is wrong is that a Shylock should be given a return on a loan when the ships of Antonio are on the rocks. But the Catholic theologians of Luther's day were evading the Thomistic ethic by devising synonyms for usury. Luther held that interest was legitimate only for the support of the aged and the infirm, incapable of production. The rate should not exceed five per cent and should be payable only if the venture had prospered. In other words, here was again the Thomistic contract of mutual risk. So also said Calvin, though he would allow the taking of interest for more than the aged and the infirm. He had on his hands thousands of religious refugees, some of whom came with money, and investment was easier to accomplish than the discovery of employment.

As for the spirit of unremitting toil, that certainly is present in Calvinism together with a disparagement of amusement. This attitude is favorable to achievement in any walk of life, whether economic or aught else. Over and over again the practice of the Christian virtues of labor, thrift, and sobriety have begotten prosperity, whether on the part of medieval monks, Anabaptist colonies, or Calvinist theocracies. Big business—buccaneering capitalism—is descended more nearly from the great banking houses of the Renaissance, and if Calvinism ever said that prosperity is the reward or the proof of God's favor, at that point it had ceased to be Calvinism. Frowning upon self-indulgence in the expenditure of money is, however, characteristic. One finds it in the attenuated Calvinism of that Scot, Andrew Carnegie, who, in the days of his fabulous wealth, allowed himself but one private luxury, a pipe-organ in his home, and this not without a sense of guilt.

**Marriage and Culture.** In the field of domestic relations the Renaissance, not Protestantism nor the Catholic Reformation, wedded romance and marriage. During the Middle Ages marriage was sacramental, rather than romantic. It was a sacrament of the Church, a lifelong relationship, with the primary purpose of propagation and the secondary intent of restraining sin by confining passion to the marital bond. Marriages were arranged by families and served also to secure and hold together estates and kingdoms. A romantic attachment between the parties was irrelevant. The cult of love began outside of marriage in the courts of love in Southern France. It was the cult of adultery. It differed from plain irregularity in that it exalted love not as a sickness or a sin but as an ennobling passion. Romantic love was called courtly love and called for courtesy. During the age of the Renaissance in several European lands one finds this concept combined with marriage. The first step was to say that if young people fell into a romantic attachment they should not enjoy physical relations until after marriage. This position one finds in Shakespeare's "Tempest" where Prospero instructs Ferdinand and Miranda that they are not to bed before they wed. The next stage was to require that the parties should have fallen in love as a prerequisite for marriage. This is the common view in the modern West and has been tacitly assumed by Catholics and Protestants alike.

But the characteristic contribution of Protestanism to the marriage relationship is quite different and comes not from Luther, who was still basically medieval. His one great change was the exaltation of marriage above virginity. The sects and Calvinism rather introduced the new view that propagation and the channeling of passion are subordinate to the mutual dedication of both partners to the service of God in the rearing of children and the maintenance of the true religion. Here is a partnership based on a common faith and a common commitment. In modern secularized form this may mean that the couple should have common interests whether in music, literature, or hobbies or what not. The idea of comradeship in marriage stems out of heroic Protestantism.

As to whether, in general, Catholicism and Protestantism are congenial to culture and the one more than the other, this is a large and illusive subject. Suffice it here to say that Christianity itself interposes a certain qualification, perhaps on opposition, at any rate a tension, to the cultivated man who seeks to round out his personality by the acquisition of all possible skills, the learning of all possible knowledge, the enjoyment, insofar as may be possible, of earth's abundant delights. Christianity demands renunciation for the sake of the neighbor and the renunciation may have to be of skills, knowledge, and enjoyment. Albert Schweitzer is the most striking example in our day of the combination of the cultivated man and the Christian man. He is distinguished as a musician, a theologian, and a physician. Scarcely in our time have we had such a revival of the Renaissance man embracing multifarious disciplines; yet Schweitzer renounced supreme attainment as an artist and even as a theologian in order to take medicine to the natives of Africa. He retains skills which dazzle the less gifted, yet he has made renunciations. Christianity can never endorse culture as an ultimate, and a culture which regards itself as ultimate will end on the futile.

# Part II

# READINGS

# LUTHER'S EARLY DEVELOPMENT[1]

*The contemporary sources for Luther's early theological development are to be found chiefly in his lectures on the Psalms (1513-15), on the Epistle to the Romans (1515-16) and again on the Psalms (1519-21) from which excerpts are here given. Almost equally important are the lectures on Hebrews and Galatians. Later in his life in various works Luther reviewed his early development. Of such statements some samples are here given.*

✓           ✓           ✓

### I. Distress in the Cloister—
### Passages from 1534, 1538-40, 1539

Luther said: I was always thinking, when will you do enough that God may be gracious? Such thoughts drove me to the monastery. . . . I went into the cloister that I might not be lost but might have eternal life. I wanted to help myself through the cowl. . . . In the cloister we had enough to eat and drink but we had suffering and torment in heart and conscience. . . . I was often terrified at the name of Jesus. The sight of a crucifix was like lightning to me and when his name was spoken I would rather have heard that of the devil, because I thought I must do good works until Christ because of them became friendly and gracious to me. I was not troubled about women, gold, and goods but I had lost faith and could not suppose that God was other than angry, and that I must placate him with my good deeds.

[1] The passages cited in this reading are from the Weimar edition of Luther's works in the following order: (I) 37, p. 661; 47, p. 84; 47, p. 589; 4, p. 43. (II) 56, pp. 207, 250-51, 380-81, 391-92, 417, 423. (III) 5, pp. 603-07. (IV) 4, p. 204; 54, p. 185; 32, p. 328.

## II. The Condition of Man—from the Lectures on Romans (1515-16)

The whole purpose of the apostle, as of his Lord, is to humble the proud, to teach them their need of grace, to destroy their own justice, and drive them in humility to Christ, that they may confess themselves sinners, receive grace and be saved. . . . Unless a man learns to listen freely to that which goes against him, unless he rejoices to have his own intent thwarted and reproved, again unless he is unhappy or at least disquieted when his own word, way and work are lauded and extolled, he cannot be saved. . . . Everything from God is rejected of man. All the prophets were persecuted because their words were unpalatable. Wherefore the Lord said, "Woe unto you when men speak well of you." (*Luke 6:26.*) Therefore to be despised, reviled and rejected is the way of security. To be blessed, praised and approved is the way of danger and perdition. . . . Because God hides His power in weakness, His wisdom in folly, His tenderness in harshness, His mercy in wroth. He answers us in a way clean contrary to our notions. We ask to be saved and He in order that He may save first damns, just as when He was about to deliver Israel, first He hardened Pharoah's heart against them and seemed to intend nothing so little as their deliverance. . . . Nobody knows whether he loves God purely unless he would be willing not to be saved but rather to be damned if it so pleased God. The damned are tortured because they are not willing to be damned, nor resign themselves to this will of God, nor can they without grace. This appears to me to be the pain of purgatory that souls imperfect in love dread this resignation. The saints abound so in love toward God that they would be willing to endure hell. Therefore they at once escape this penalty. There is no fear that they will be damned, because freely and in love they accept damnation for God's sake. They rather are damned who flee damnation. . . . The popes and prelates who for the temporal goods of the Church dispense indulgences are cruel to the uttermost if they would not do more or as much freely for God on behalf of souls, for that which is freely received should be freely given. They are seduced and seduce the people from the true worship of God. . . . The word of God when it comes is counter to our mind and wish. An infallible sign that one truly has the word of God is that one should find nothing pleasing in oneself, for the word of God destroys and crucifies and leaves in us nothing save that which is displeasing, that our pleasure, joy, and trust should be in God alone.

### III. The Grace of God in the Death of Christ— from Lectures on the Psalms (1519-21)

Christ was just and remained just. He did no sin, "neither was any guile found in his mouth" . . . yet in his passion he took to himself our sins as if they were his own. He endured everything which we ought to have endured for our sins. As Isaiah said (*Chapter 53*) "surely he hath borne our grief and carried our sorrow; for the sins of my people he was stricken." This being stricken by God is not only the penalty of death but also the fear and horror of the anguished conscience which feels the divine anger and even though in eternity would feel itself forsaken and cast away from the presence of God. . . . Wherefore Paul said that Christ for us became accursed. (*Galatians 3:13*.) . . . But is it not absurd to attribute to Christ even for a moment a troubled conscience on account of our misery when he himself was innocent? . . . He differed greatly from us. . . . In him there was no sin as there is in us. It is not without murmur and blasphemy that we cry "My God, my God, why hast Thou forsaken me?" On Christ's lips the cry was neither murmur nor blasphemy. . . . He still loved the Father utterly but the pangs, exceeding his strength, drove his innocent and weak nature to groan, cry, shudder and flee just as without sin he sank beneath the weight of the cross. The cry "my God, my God" was like blasphemy but it was not. Some may object that it certainly indicates discord between the will of Christ and the will of God. That would have been true had we been in his place. . . . Nevertheless we are not to deny that Christ was terrified and tormented like the damned when they tremble and flee from God. Christ in his own eyes was like them, a derelict, accursed, a sinner, a blasphemer and damned, even though he was without sin and guilt. It was no make-believe that cry

"My God, my God." This should be a comfort to those who are vexed by the abyss to the gate of death lest they despair and a warning to those who walk upon the clouds and make their nests among the stars, lest they presume. . . . Observe now that when God was far He was at the same time near. He was far because Christ used the word "forsaken," He was near because Christ said *"My* God."

## IV. Justification by Faith

A. *First Glimmerings in 1513.* We are not justified by works but just works proceed from the just . . . [*commenting on Psalm 106, 3: "Blessed are they that keep judgment."*] He who keeps judgment is he who is always destroying himself according to the old man, and he who keeps justification is he who is always building himself up according to the new man, but it is arduous to keep judgment, a constant battle because it means holding oneself to true humility and subjection, to resignation of one's own will and counsel. In German it is called *Herzbrechen,* a breaking of the heart. A most noble virtue it is to which the wicked do not attain because they are always excusing, justifying and defending themselves.

B. *The full disclosure* [*passages composed in 1545 and 1532*]: I greatly longed to understand Paul's Epistle to the Romans and nothing stood in the way but that one expression, "the justice of God," because I took it to mean that justice whereby God is just and deals justly in punishing the unjust. My situation was that, although an impeccable monk, I stood before God as a sinner troubled in conscience, and I had no confidence that my merit would assuage him. Therefore I did not love a just and angry God, but rather hated and murmured against Him. Yet I clung to the dear Paul and had a great yearning to know what he meant.

Night and day I pondered until I saw the connection between the justice of God and the statement that "the just shall live by his faith." Then I grasped that the justice of God is that righteousness by which through grace and sheer mercy God justifies us through faith. Thereupon I felt myself to be reborn and to have gone through open doors into paradise. The whole of Scripture took on a new meaning, and whereas before the "justice of God" had filled me with hate, now it became to be inexpressibly sweet in greater love. This passage of Paul became to me a gate to heaven. . . .

If you have a true faith that Christ is your Saviour, then at once you have a gracious God, for faith leads you in and opens up God's heart and will, that you should see pure grace and overflowing love. This it is to behold God in faith that you should look upon His fatherly, friendly heart, in which there is no anger nor ungraciousness. He who sees God as angry does not see Him rightly but looks only on a curtain, as if a dark cloud had been drawn across his face.

# — Reading No. 2 —

## THE INDULGENCE CONTROVERSY AND LUTHER'S PROPOSALS FOR PRACTICAL REFORM[2]

*Luther was drawn into the arena of reform by his objection to the practice of indulgences. The particular instance lay in the instructions of Albert of Mainz to the vendors of indulgences in his territories. Albert's pretensions on behalf of the indulgence were the most extravagant ever made. Luther's* Ninety-Five Theses *were*

[1] The documents in this reading are taken from (I) Walther Koehler, *Dokumente zum Ablassstreit* (2nd ed., Tübingen, 1934), Dok. 31, greatly condensed; (II) *Ibid.*, Dok. 33, greatly condensed; (III) Luther's Works, Erlangen Ed., *Opera Latina varii argumenti* 1, pp. 344-47; (IV) Luther's Two Replies to Prierias, 1518 and 1520; (A) Weimar ed., 1, pp. 656-57, 662, 678-79; Erlangen ed., *Opera Latina varii argumenti* 2, pp. 22, 31, 54-56; (B) Weimar ed., 6, pp. 328-29; Erlangen v.a. 2, pp. 79-81; (V) Bonn ed., edited by Otto Clemen.

*an attack upon this document. They can be found in
English translation in full in many places, among others
in the* Works of Martin Luther *(A. J. Holman Co.,
Philadelphia, 1915), vol. 1, pp. 25-38. The reply to
Luther by Sylvester Prierias lifted the controversy to a
new level by its assertion of papal authority, and Luther
in his two replies dwarfed the indulgence question by a
flat denial of papal and also of conciliar infallibility. In
the summer of 1520, three years after the outbreak of
the controversy, Luther issued several great manifestoes
of reform, of which one was* The Address to the Nobility
of the German Nation. *This deals largely with the moral
and financial abuses of the Church. The appeal is addressed in medieval fashion to the civil arm of a Christian
society to redress the offenses of the spiritual. Luther's
doctrine of the priesthood of all believers supports his
appeal to the lay rulers. This work is translated in full
in the work referred to above.*

*Both the* Theses *and the* Address *are translated in
Bertram Lee Woolf,* Reformation Writings of Martin
Luther, *vol. 1 (London, 1952).*

✓          ✓          ✓

## I. The *Instructions* of Albert of Mainz
to the Indulgence Preachers, 1517

Inasmuch as the Church of Peter and Paul, the head
of all the churches, was razed by the order of Pope
Julius II of pious memory, we intend to construct a new
edifice surpassing every other. Since the bones of Peter
and Paul and innumerable saints on this spot are subject
to constant desecration of rain and hail and since the
entire resources of the Roman See are inadequate to
finish this magnificent project, his Holiness has been
prompted by God to stir up the faithful to this end by
offering them these indulgences which are the peculiar
treasury of Saint Peter.

Four graces are conceded in this indulgence. The first
is the plenary remission of all sins and that the pains of
purgatory are completely remitted. In order the more
readily to induce contributions the preachers should
propose a graduated scale. Kings, queens, and their sons,
archbishops and bishops, and other great magnates
should give at least twenty-five gold Rhenish florins.

Abbots, prelates of cathedral churches, counts, barons and other great nobles and their wives should give ten (and so on). . . . Those who have no money may contribute by prayers and fasting, for the kingdom of heaven belongs no less to the poor than to the rich. The second grace is that once later in life and in the hour of death there is granted a plenary indulgence of even the gravest sins. The third is participation in all the benefits of the Church, that is, in the benefits accruing from all the prayers, fasts, pilgrimages and alms in the universal holy Church militant. The fourth is that a plenary remission of all sins is given to souls in purgatory. This the Pope grants by way of intercession. There is no need that those who contribute on behalf of these souls should themselves be contrite and confessed.

II. Luther's *Ninety-five Theses*, October 31, 1517

(5) The Pope does not wish and cannot remit any penalties save those which he has himself imposed.

(8) The penitential canons are imposed only on the living.

(21) Those indulgence preachers are wrong who say that the Pope can remit every penalty.

(27-28) They say, "As soon as the coin in the coffer rings the soul from purgatory springs." What "springs" out is the spirit of avarice.

(29) Who knows whether the souls in purgatory wish to be released?

(30) No one is certain as to his contrition.

(40) Genuine contrition seeks and loves penalties.

(45) Christians should be taught that he who neglects the needy in order to secure pardons earns not the indulgence of the Pope but the indignation of God.

(50) If the Pope knew the exactions of the venal preachers, he would prefer that the Basilica of St. Peter should lie in ashes rather than that it should be built out of the hide, flesh and bones of his sheep.

(56) The treasury of the Church from which the Pope grants indulgences (58) is not the merits of Christ and the saints because these always and without the Pope bring grace to the inward man and the cross, death and hell to the outward man.

(62) The true treasury of the Church is the most holy gospel of the glory and grace of God.

(66) The treasury of indulgences is a net for catching the riches of men.

(82) If the Pope is willing to release infinite souls from purgatory on account of filthy gain, for the trivial purpose of building a basilica, why does he not empty the place out of most holy love and the most just of all purposes, namely the supreme need of souls?

(86) Why doesn't he build the Basilica of St. Peter out of his own money seeing that he is richer than Croesus?

(94) Christians should be taught to seek Christ, their head, through mortification, death and hell.

## III. The Reply of Prierias

*The Pope commissioned the Dominican, Sylvester Prierias, to reply to Luther. In December, 1517 he brought out his* Dialogue Concerning the Power of the Pope.

The universal Church is essentially the gathering in divine worship of all those believing in Christ. The universal Church indeed is virtually the Roman Church, the head of all the churches and the Pope. The Roman Church consists representatively in the college of cardinals, virtually however in the Pope, who is the head of the Church, in a different sense however than Christ. As the universal Church is not able to err in determining faith and morals, so also a true council . . . is not able to err. . . . Likewise neither is the Roman church nor the Pope able to err when acting in his official capacity as Pope. . . . He who does not accept the doctrine of the Roman Church and of the Roman pontiff as the infallible rule of faith from which sacred Scripture draws its strength and authority is a heretic. The Roman Church is able to determine not only in word but also in deed concerning faith and morals. . . . Wherefore, just as he is a heretic who thinks incorrectly concerning the truth of the Scriptures, so also is he who thinks wrongly concerning the doctrine and the deeds of the Church in matters of faith and morals. The corollary is that whoever says that the Roman Church is not able to do in the matter of indulgences what actually she does is a heretic.

### IV. Luther's Two *Replies to Prierias,* 1518 and 1520

A. *The Reply of 1518:* The Roman Church, you say, is representatively the cardinals and virtually the Pope. I reply that the Pope can err and a council can err. . . . I would say that the Church is virtually Christ and representatively a council. If you are right that what the Pope does the Church does, I ask you what abomination will you not have to regard as deeds of the Church? Look at the ghastly bloodshed of Julius II, the abominable tyrannies of Boniface VIII, of whom it was said that he entered as a wolf, ran as a lion and died as a dog. You will not persuade us that such atrocious abuses are deeds of the most holy Church. We Germans suspect that you have written not so much to refute Martin as to adulate the Pope and the cardinals. If the Pope is the virtual Church and the cardinals the representative Church what do you make of a council? . . . I reject your view that Peter can loose what God has bound. . . . I marvel that you make no appeal to Scripture. For me Augustine is greater than St. Thomas and Paul is my foundation. I marvel that you call the Roman Church the rule of faith. I always supposed that faith is the rule of the Roman Church and of all the churches. . . . Our basilicas are of more use to us than St. Peter's which we cannot attend. Better that St. Peter's should never be built than that our parochial churches should be wrecked. We regret that all the revenues of the churches are sucked into the insatiable Basilica of St. Peter's. . . . You alleged that if the Pope would give me a bishopric endowed with a plenary indulgence for the repair of my church I would abound in sweet words. If I aspired to a bishopric I would not say what you hear with such impatience. Don't you think I know that the very boys in the streets sing about the way bishoprics are obtained at Rome? . . . I know we have an excellent Pope, Leo X [*The Lion*]. He is like Daniel at Babylon [*in the den of lions*] by his innocence in danger of his very life [*referring to a plot among the cardinals to assassinate the Pope*].

B. *The Second Reply:* If what you say is held and taught with the knowledge of the Pope and the cardinals, which I hope is not the case, then I say flatly that in these writings the very Anti-Christ sits in the temple of God and the Roman Curia is the synagogue of Satan. What shall I say? Prierias makes even an impious Pope into a god and derives the authority of Holy Scripture from that man however unworthy, whereas all agree that the authority of the Pope is derived from Christ. . . . And now this Satan fortifies Scripture through a man. What is Anti-Christ if such a Pope is not? . . . Weep, reader, that the glory of Rome is so far fallen that such heretical, blasphemous, diabolical and hellish poison is not only nurtured but propagated at Rome. If this is what Rome believes, blessed are the Greeks, the Bohemians and those separated from this Babylon. And if this is what the Pope and the cardinals teach, then I confess that I dissent from the Roman Church and reject it together with the Pope and the cardinals as the abomination standing in the holy place.

## V. *The Address to the Christian Nobility of the German Nation,* August, 1520

[*Luther begins by suggesting that a new Joshua is about to blow down the walls of the Jericho at Rome.*] The First wall is that the spiritual is above the civil power, the second is that only the Pope is able to interpret the Scripture, and the third is that no one can call a council except the Pope. . . . As for the first, all Christians are truly of the spiritual estate and there is no difference among them except as to their office. . . . Through baptism we are all ordained to the priesthood. . . . When a bishop ordains it is simply that one person is selected to exercise for the rest the power in which all share. To illustrate, if a little group of Christians were taken into exile where there was no ordained priest and if they were to elect one of their number, married or unmarried, they could confer on him authority to baptize, say mass, absolve, and preach, and he would be as true a priest as if ordained by all the bishops and popes. . . . And since the civil rulers have the same baptism as we, the same faith in the Gospel, we must regard them as priests and bishops. But although we are all priests, we are not to assume the office without the commission of the congregation, and if anyone is deposed, he is in the same status as he was before because a priest in a Christian church is nothing but an office-holder.

Since the civil power is ordained of God, it should not be impeded throughout Christendom in the exercise of its office though it apply to pope, bishop, priest, monk, or nun. ... . If a priest is killed the land is laid under an interdict [*an excommunication applying to an entire area*] and why not if a peasant is murdered? Whence arises such a difference among Christians, if not from the laws of men?

The second wall is even more flimsy that the papists claim to be the sole interpreters of the Holy Scriptures. ... . If that were so, what need would there be for the Holy Scriptures? Let us burn them and rely on the un-learned lords at Rome who have the Holy Spirit. ... . The clause in the creed would have to be altered "I believe in one Holy Christian Church" to read "I believe in the Pope at Rome," and thus reduce the Church to one single man. ... . If God through Balaam's ass spoke against the prophet, should He not be able to speak through a godly man against the Pope?

The third wall falls because the council referred to in the Book of Acts in the fifteenth chapter was called not by Peter but by all the apostles and elders. Consequently if necessity demands and the Pope is an offense to Christendom, then the first who can, should try as a true member of the whole body to bring together a truly free council which none can better do than the civil rulers because they too with us are fellow Christians, fellow priests, and fellow "spirituals."

We may now look at the matters which may properly be taken up in a council. ... . To begin with, it is shocking to see the head of Christendom, who boasts himself as the vicar of Christ and successor of Peter, living in such worldly pomp that no king or emperor can touch him. He has a three-layer crown whereas the highest king has but one. If that is like Christ and Peter, it is a new kind of likeness. [*There follows an account of the extravagance of the cardinals.*] The cardinals have sucked Italy dry and now turn to Germany. ... . I propose that the number of cardinals be reduced or that the Pope be forced to maintain them himself. . . . If the Pope's court were reduced, ninety-nine per cent, it would still be large enough to give decisions in matters of faith. Annates [*a tax of one half of the first year's income of a newly appointed bishop*] are levied ostensibly for crusades against the Turks which never come off. The money goes into a bottomless bag. When the Pope rides out he is accompanied by three or four thousand mule riders beyond any emperor or king. Christ and Peter had to go on foot in order that their vicar might the better swagger. . . . The overweening, lying, reservation [*the reserving of appeals to Rome*] of the popes has made Rome unspeakable. . . . The reign of Anti-Christ could not be worse.

Recommendations: Every prince, noble, and city should strictly forbid their subjects to pay annates to Rome. . . . No civil case should be appealed to Rome. . . . Ecclesiastical cases should be referred to the Primate of Germany. The Pope has no authority over the Emperor who should not yield to devilish arrogance and kiss the Pope's toe. Pilgrimages should be abolished. The money might much better be given to the poor. But if anybody wishes simply to see the world, let him go. Priests should be free to marry. There is many a worthy priest against whom there is nothing except that he has come to shame with a woman when both of them desire in their hearts to live faithfully in holy wedlock, if only they could do so in good conscience. All holy days should be given up and Sunday alone observed. . . . By what authority does the Pope canonize the saints? Let them canonize themselves. Public begging should be forbidden throughout Christendom. Let each town support its own poor. I will not pass judgment on the writings of John Hus [*a Bohemian heretic executed in 1415*] though so far I have found in them no errors. In any case heretics should be overcome with writings, not with fire. If fire were the way, the executioners would be the greatest doctors on earth. There would be no need to study, but he who could overcome another by force might burn him. The Pope should permit the Bohemians to choose for themselves an Archbishop of Prague.

## — Reading No. 3 —

# LUTHER'S REVISION
## OF THE SACRAMENTS[3]

The Babylonian Captivity *which followed by one
month the* Address to Nobility *was at once deemed the
most radical of all Luther's utterances because it largely
demolished the Church's sacramental system on which
rested so much else. One may plausibly assume that the
examiner of Luther at the Diet of Worms was giving
him an opportunity to disclaim this work. First he was
asked whether he had actually written all of the books
which had appeared under his name. When he acknowledged them all he was asked whether he would defend
all that he had said in them. If he had renounced what
he had said on the sacraments the other points of his
attack would have been open to discussion. This tract is
translated in full in the* Works of Martin Luther (*A. J.*
Holman Co., *Philadelphia, 1915*), vol. II, pp. 170-293.
The Freedom of the Christian Man *is pp. 301-348.*

*Though Luther's attack on the sacraments was con-
sidered the most drastic he was popularly charged with
demolishing also the Christian ethic by eliminating the
motive of reward. In* The Freedom of the Christian Man
*he rebuilt ethics on the basis of gratitude and devotion.
Both of the works in this section are translated in Bertram Lee Woolf,* Reformation Writings of Martin Luther,
vol. I (*London, 1952*).

✓          ✓          ✓

### I. *The Babylonian Captivity,* September, 1520

To begin with, I must deny that there are seven sacraments. For the moment I would assume three: baptism,
penance and the bread and all of these have been carried
by the Roman Church into dire captivity.

**The Sacrament of the Bread.** *Communion in both
kinds:* If the Church is able to withhold the wine from

[3] Bonn ed., edited by Clemen, 1, pp. 491-510.

the laity, she might also withhold the bread and thus
completely abnegate the institution of Christ. . . . The
most important evidence to my mind is that Christ said,
"This is my blood which is shed for you and for many
for the remission of sins." Here you see most clearly
that the blood is to be given to those for whose sins it
has been shed. *Transubstantiation:* Years ago I was im-
pressed by the statement of Cardinal Pierre D'Ailly that
it would be much simpler and more probable to assume
that real bread and real wine were on the altar and not
mere accidents had not the Church ruled otherwise.
When I came to see that the Church which so ruled was
the Thomistic, that is the Aristotelian church, I became
bolder because I saw that Thomistic opinions, even
though approved by the Pope or a council, remained
only opinions and not articles of faith, for what is asserted without the authority of Scripture or an approved
revelation may be opined but need not be believed. . . .
The Church believed correctly for more than twelve
hundred years and during that time the holy fathers never
once mentioned the preposterous word for a monstrous
idea, transubstantiation, introduced only when the
pseudo-philosophy of Aristotle ran riot in the Church.
. . . Why should not Christ contain his body in the substance as well as in the accidents of the bread? just as
fire and iron, two substances, are so mingled when red
hot that each is iron and fire. Let us not meddle too
much with philosophy. If I cannot grasp how the bread
is the body of Christ, I will subject my understanding
to obedience to Christ and hold simply to his word. I
believe firmly not only that the body of Christ is in the
bread but that the bread is the body of Christ. . . . For
the godhead to be incarnated in him, it was not necessary
that his human nature be transubstantiated. . . . Likewise
in the sacrament it is not necessary that bread and wine be
transubstantiated in order to be the true body and the
true blood. What we call the Mass is a promise of the
forgiveness of sins made to us by God and confirmed by
the death of His son. A faith holding faithfully to this
promise is all that is needed in order to hold the Mass
worthily. There follows unprompted from this state a
most sweet welling of the heart, whereby the spirit of
man is enlarged and waxes fat. He is drawn to Christ

and becomes utterly a new man. Who would not weep sweetly and almost faint for joy in Christ if he really believed that this inestimable promise actually applied to him? . . . But our theologians have become immersed in infinite metaphysical quibbles.

*A Good Work:* The doctrines of impious men have converted the Mass into a good work. . . . It cannot possibly be a good work. There is nothing to be worked. It operates only by faith and faith is not a work but the lord and life of all works. The Mass is a divine promise which can profit none, apply to none, intercede for none, and be communicated to none unless he believes with his own faith. How can the promise of God which demands faith individually of everyone be accepted or applied by one on behalf of another? Am I able to give the promise of God to another if he does not believe? Can I believe for another? Can I make him believe? . . . This invincible truth must stand. Where there is a divine promise, there each must stand for himself, believe for himself and answer for himself. . . . But you say, would you undercut the very basis of so many churches and monasteries for they base their anniversaries, intercessions, etc., that is, their fat intake on the Mass? Precisely! That is what I call the Babylonian Captivity. . . . I readily concede that the prayers which those congregated for the Mass say on behalf of each other are good works in the sense of benefits . . . but does any priest when he sacrifices think that he is offering nothing more than prayers? . . . God alone gives the Mass to those men who accept it in faith, in faith alone, without works and without merits.

*A Sacrifice:* The Mass is held to be a sacrifice offered to God. . . . To this we must oppose the words and the example of Christ, for unless we hold the Mass to be a promise we shall lose the whole Gospel and our solace. A promise is simply accepted. A sacrifice has to be offered, and it is not possible at the same moment both to give and receive the Mass. The testament or promise of Christ is the only cure for the sad, afflicted, perturbed, confused and erring consciences. He who does not believe will never by any works or effort be able to appease his conscience. Faith alone brings peace.

*Baptism:* The first point in Baptism is the divine

promise, "He who believes and is baptized shall be saved.". . . Unless one believes, Baptism is of no avail. . . . One must begin with the faith of the sacraments without any works whatsoever. . . . The efficacy of baptism resides not in him who confers it but in him who receives in faith and use. . . . Baptism signifies death and resurrection, that is full and complete justification. . . . Not that sin completely dies before the body of sin which we carry in this life is destroyed but as soon as we believe we begin to die to this world. . . . Sacramentally we are baptized only once, but in faith constantly because we must always die and always live. . . . Baptism must occupy us body and soul all our lives until we are clothed in the robe of immortality.

*Infant Baptism:* In view of the above some may object that infants should not be baptized because they cannot grasp the promise, cannot have faith, and therefore either faith is not required or else babies should not be baptized. I reply that they are sustained by the faith of the sponsors through the prayers of the faithful in the church. The child is changed, cleansed, and renewed through an infused faith.

*Vows:* One more point. I should like to abolish all vows completely, whether vows to become monks, to go on pilgrimages or anything else. . . . We have vowed enough in our baptism and more than we can fulfill. . . . We fill the world with priests, monks, and nuns and lock them up in perpetual vows. Some even say that to enter a religious order constitutes a new baptism. . . . Not that I would go so far as to impede a free and private vow, but I absolutely disapprove of institutionalizing vows into a public way of life. . . . There is no example in Scripture of a perpetual vow of poverty, chastity, and obedience. I would not persuade and would vehemently dissuade anyone from entering an order or becoming a priest unless he recognizes that what he does, however rugged, counts no more in the eyes of God than the work of a farmer in the field or a *Hausfrau* in the home, because the eyes of the Lord look only onto faith.

*Penance:* The trouble with this sacrament is that there is not a shred of it left. It has been divided into three parts: contrition, confession, and satisfaction. Contrition is held to precede faith and thereby it becomes a merit.

. . . A contrite heart is a great thing, but it is found only where there is a burning faith in God's promises and menaces. Yet contrition has been less subject to tyranny and exploitation than to impiety. . . . But confession and satisfaction are a veritable minting house of wealth and power. There is no doubt that confession of sins is necessary and commended of God . . . and secret confession, even though not commended in Scripture, is nevertheless highly useful and necessary, but I detest the prostitution of confession to gain. Secret sins and minor sins are reserved for absolution by the ministers of the Golden Calf, but I believe that anyone is absolved of secret sins who confesses, seeks pardon and amendment of life privately from any brother. The doctrine of satisfaction has been so perverted that people do not realize that satisfaction is simply amendment of life, not pilgrimages, flagellation, mortifications, etc. To the woman taken in adultery Christ said only, "Go and sin no more."

*Confirmation:* I marvel that anyone ever got it into his head to make a sacrament out of the laying on of hands. It is enough to regard confirmation as a rite of the Church or as a sacramental ceremony.

*Marriage:* There is no Scripture for regarding marriage as a sacrament because in every sacrament there is a promise and a sign, but marriage is not instituted of God as a sign of anything. Moreover, marriage was instituted from the beginning of the world and applied to non-Christians. Therefore it cannot be specifically a sacrament of the Church. With regard to *spiritual consanguinity,* what but the superstition of men invented this? Is not every baptized man a brother to every baptized woman and could Paul not have married a girl in Corinth because he boasted that he had begotten all in Christ? . . . Between a priest and his wife there is an indissoluble marriage approved by the ordinance of God. . . . What earthly sense is there in the rule that no man can marry a widow of a deceased relative to the fourth degree? . . . As for divorce I so hate it that I would prefer bigamy.

*Ordination:* Of this sacrament the Church of Christ knows nothing. The strongest buttress adduced is that Christ said, "Do this in remembrance of me." Christ is claimed by these words to have ordained the disciples as priests, but who of the fathers ever interpreted his saying in this way? This forced exegesis has sown impossible enmity and divided the clergy and the laity as far as heaven and earth . . . to the point that those who are anointed, tonsured and vestured not only exalt themselves above lay Christians anointed by the Holy Spirit but treat them actually as dogs not fit to be counted with them in the Church. . . . If they were brought to admit that all who are baptized are equally priests, as truly we are, and that they have received their ministry solely through our consent, they would realize that they had no authority over us, save in so far as we confer it upon them. . . . We are all priests and those we call priests are ministers chosen by us to act in our name. The priesthood is nothing but a ministry and the sacrament of ordination is nothing other than a rite of choosing a preacher in the Church. . . . No one, however, is to assume this office without the consent of the community or the call of a superior.

*Extreme Unction:* If ever there were delirium, this is it.

One might include among the sacraments prayer, the word and the cross whereas strictly the term is used of promises with signs annexed and in this sense there are really but two, baptism and the bread. The sacrament of penance lacks the visible and divinely instituted sign, and as I said is only a return to baptism.

## II. On the Freedom of the Christian Man, November, 1520

The soul which with a firm faith cleaves to the promises of God is united with them, absorbed by them, penetrated, saturated, inebriated by their power. If the touch of Christ was healing, how much more does that most tender touch in the spirit, that absorption in the Word convey to the soul all the qualities of the Word so that it becomes trustworthy, peaceable, free, full of every good, a true child of God. From this we see very easily why faith can do so much and no good work is like unto it, for no good work comes from God's Word like faith. No good work can be within the soul, but the Word and faith reign there. What the Word is that the soul is, as iron becomes fire-red through union with the flame. Plainly then faith is enough for the Christian man. He has no need for works to be made just. Then is he free from the law.

But he is not therefore to be lazy or loose. Good works do not make a man good, but a good man does good works. A bishop is not a bishop because he consecrates a church, but he consecrates a church because he is a bishop. Unless a man is already a believer and a Christian, his works have no value at all. They are foolish, idle, damnable sins, because when good works are brought forward as ground for justification, they are no longer good. Understand that we do not reject good works, but praise them highly. The apostle Paul said, "Let this mind be in you which was also in Christ Jesus, who being on an equality with God emptied himself, taking the form of a servant, and becoming obedient unto death." Paul means that when Christ was fully in the form of God, abounding in all things, so that he had no need of any work or any suffering to be saved, he was not puffed up, did not arrogate to himself power, but rather in suffering, working, enduring, and dying made himself like other men, as if he needed all things and were not in the form of God. All this he did to serve us. When God in his sheer mercy and without any merit of mine has given me such unspeakable riches, shall I not then freely, joyously, wholeheartedly, unprompted do everything that I know will please him? I will give myself as a sort of Christ to my neighbor as Christ gave himself for me. . . .

I must even take to myself the sins of others as Christ took mine to himself. Thus we see that the Christian man lives not to himself but to Christ and his neighbor through love. By faith he rises above himself to God and from God goes below himself in love and remains always in God and in love.

# LUTHER AND THE SAXON RADICALS[*]

*Luther claimed that the attack by the radicals from within his own camp was more of a blow than the repudiation by the papacy. The two most outstanding leaders of the opposition were Carlstadt and Müntzer. The latter was an avowed revolutionist of violence. The former was not, but they were in touch with each other and Luther lumped them together. The passages from Carlstadt illustrate his objection to images and his spiritual interpretation of the Lord's Supper. In other works Carlstadt often appealed to the spirit versus the letter of Scripture. He would suffer no special clerical garb. Luther in his reply covers all these points.*

*Müntzer did believe that the return of the Lord Jesus should be preceded by the slaughter of the ungodly. The angels, who are to wield the sickle and cut down the tares, are primarily the elect who follow the spirit rather than the letter of the Scripture and are ready to suffer like the crucified Christ. They may enlist the help of the willing. Müntzer appealed first to the Humanists. They were deaf. Then he called on the Saxon princes, hinting that they should accord him the role of the prophet Daniel as interpreter of the dreams of King Nebuchad-*

[*] The documents in this reading are taken from (I) Andreas Bodenstein von Karlstadt, "Von Abtuung der Bilder," ed. Hans Lietzmann, *Kleine Texte* 74 (Bonn, 1911); (II) *Von dem widerchristlichen Missbrauch des Herrn Brod und Kelch,* St. Louis edition of Luther's Works (reprint of the Walch edition with different pagination), XX, pp. 93-109; (III) Thomas Müntzer, *Von dem gedichteten Glauben;* and (IV) *Die Fürstenpredigt* both in Otto Brandt, *Thomas Müntzer, sein Leben und seine Schriften* (1933); (V) Luther, *Wider die himmlischen Propheten,* Weimar ed., XVIII, pp. 62-202; (VI) Karlstadt, St. Louis edition of Luther's Works, XX, pp. 286-311.

*nezzar. The princes banished Müntzer. His final appeal was to the peasants who heeded, took the sword and perished, Müntzer with them. Luther's tract* Against the Heavenly Prophets *was directed primarily against Carlstadt. In other writings he was even more virulent against Müntzer.*

✓          ✓          ✓

## I. Carlstadt: *On the Removal of the Images*, 1522

To have images in churches is contrary to the first commandment, "Thou shalt have no other gods before me." To place idols on altars is even more devilish. Therefore, we should put them away in obedience to Scripture. We cannot deny that we love the images, otherwise we would not have bedecked them with silk and damask, gold and silver, with crowns and jewels which we cannot afford for our children, wives, parents, and princes. God will say to us, "How have you become so impudent as to bow and scrape in My house before images and give them the honor due unto Me?" I must confess that everything which God said against the idolatry of Jews applies to our pretended Christians who seek help and counsel from images and are themselves blinder than the ox at Leipzig.

God said, "Thou shalt not make unto thee any graven image, or any likeness of any thing that is in heaven above, or that is in the earth beneath, or that is in the water under the earth. Thou shalt not bow down thyself to them nor serve them." [*Genesis 20:4-5.*] If anyone says, "I do not praise the images. I honor them not for their own sake, but for the saints whom they represent," then God answers straightway, "Thou shalt not bow down to them." Gloss that as you will, it says outright, "Thou shalt not bow down, thou shalt not bend a knee or light a candle." God says, "If I had wished you to worship Me or My saints through images I would not have forbidden you to make an image or a likeness." Pope Gregory said that images are the books of the laity. Is not that a regular popish trick? Moses said, "You should teach your children God's word from their youth up." What can the laity learn from pictures unless it be to esteem the physical? For example, from the Crucifix you learn only the physical suffering of Christ, how He drooped His head, etc. But Christ said, "The flesh profiteth nothing and only the spirit makes alive." [*John 6:63.*]

Those who disobey God must die the death. With groans I will freely confess my secret thoughts before the world and disclose that I am weak. I know that we are commanded to fear no image, but God counts with me for so little that I do fear them, but God wants my whole heart and cannot suffer that I have an image before my eyes. Josiah burned the images of Baal and our magistrates should not wait for the priests of Baal (that is, the priests of the Church of Rome) to leave the cloisters. They will never make a start. The magistrate should take a hand.

### II. Carlstadt: *On the Unchristian Abuse of the Lord's Body and of the Cup,* September, 1524

I, Andreas Bodenstein von Carlstadt, must openly proclaim that many Christians are taking the body and the cup to their hurt. Although others should have undertaken this proclamation, namely the princes of the Scribes, yet because they hide behind the bush, I must step forth and confess God's truth and Christ's righteousness, though it cost me my life. . . . The sacrament of the bread does not accomplish the forgiveness of sins. The Lord said, "This do in *remembrance* of me." Now remembrance is a burning, living way of knowing the body and blood of Christ. No one can conceive of it who has not known it. This is not a frozen dead knowledge, but a warm, burning, active and powerful work of Christ which transforms him who knows it into the life and death of Christ, that for Christ's sake he will do or suffer whatever Christ wills. Beware lest you make mere flesh out of the Lord's body and blood. These profit nothing. You must have before your eyes the great invisible love, the exceeding obedience, the amazing innocence of Christ. You must grasp this in the depth of your heart, then are you justified and free from sin. From the knowing of Christ arises the remembrance of Christ. Not a raw, cold, tepid remembrance, but a fresh and mighty remembrance with joy that cherishes the body laid down and the blood of Christ shed which gives thanks and becomes Christ-like and shames whatever is against him. Suppose you had been condemned to death by the gallows, wheel, or fire and someone came, ready to die for you and let you go free. Would not you be ashamed if you ever failed to love such a friend and would you not be glad if his name were mentioned, and if he had left something to be done in his remembrance would you not do it?

### III. Thomas Müntzer: *The Concocted Faith,* 1524

Dear Christians: The Scripture is a two-edged sword which kills rather than makes alive, unlike the living word. Let us then not take a passage here or a passage there but gather all together in the teaching of the spirit rather than of the flesh. One must listen to the voice of a teacher like John the Baptist in the wilderness that one may be ready to receive the source of blessedness, the Son of God, who as a lamb before the shearers was dumb and opened not his mouth. Preaching of a sweet Christ to a carnal world is the worst poison. He who will not have a bitter Christ will kill himself on honey. We must go through desperation and contraries. One who is learned according to men cannot understand the Scriptures but must wait for the key of David till he is truly crushed, and has no wish other than that he desires faith. We must follow in the footsteps of Christ. This was the teaching of the Abbot Joachim called "The Eternal Gospel," commonly derided but by me esteemed, though I learned not from him, but was taught from above.

### IV. Thomas Müntzer: *The Sermon to the Princes,* 1524

King Nebuchadnezzar had a dream: The Word must come down from God into our stupefied heart and he who is not receptive to the inner Word in the abyss of his soul knows nothing of God though he may have swallowed one hundred thousand bibles. An elect man who would know the meaning of a dream or vision, whether it be of God, of nature, or of the devil, must be free in feeling, heart and natural understanding from all temporal comfort of the flesh. God sends dreams and visions to his beloved friends, particularly in times of great trouble. It is a true apostolic, patriarchal, and prophetic spirit to wait upon dreams and it is no wonder that brother Fat Hog and Plush Liver (*Luther*) rejects them.

I know it for true that the Spirit of God has revealed to many elect and godly men an overwhelming coming Reformation to be accomplished as Daniel foresaw at the end of the fifth monarchy. Therefore, you princes of Saxony, stand upon the rock like Peter. A new prophet must arise and declare unto you the revelation. The wrath of the princes must be kindled. Christ said that he came not to bring peace but a sword, and again He said, "Take my enemies and slay them before my eyes." [*Luke 19:27.*] Think not that you can let your sword rust in the scabbard. God says, "Thou shalt not suffer an evil doer to live." [*Exodus 22:18, a witch.*] This will cost you a great cross and acute distress as David was driven out by Absolem, yet was able later to return. God requires that you destroy all of the images, when He says, "You are a holy people." [*Deuteronomy 7:5-6.*] The sword is necessary to wipe out the godless; it must be wielded by the princes who with us are fellow Christians and if they refuse, the sword shall be taken from them. Hezekiah, Josiah, Cyrus, Daniel and Elias destroyed the priests of Baal. The tares must be rooted from the vineyard of the Lord in the time of the harvest and the angels who put in the sickle are the servants of God. Godless rulers, particularly priests and monks, are to be killed. Remember that Nebuchadnezzar harkened unto Daniel and appointed him to administer justice. The godless have no right to live, save as the elect may concede it to them. Be bold. He will have the rule to whom power is given in heaven and on earth. May He ever keep you, beloved.

### V. Luther: *Against the Heavenly Prophets With Regard to Images and the Sacraments,* February, 1525

Carlstadt has fallen away from us and has become our worst enemy. We have had to deal with false prophets for now these three years. With regard to images, before Carlstadt dreamed of smashing them I said that we should take the images from our hearts. Then they would not hurt our eyes. He reverses this and takes them from our eyes and leaves them in our hearts. I said, if we taught the people that only faith and not images are pleasing to God they would stop making them, but if we think we please God by smashing them we have set up a new idol in the heart. What is more, I did not say that images might not be removed, provided it were done without violence and through the civil authorities. Besides Moses forbade only an image of God and not a crucifix or an image of a saint. The First Commandment says, "Thou shalt not have any gods before me." It says also, "Thou shalt not make unto thee any graven image or any likeness," etc. [*Exodus 20:3-4.*] The primary sense of the whole passage is that images of God are not to be worshipped, but these Carlstadters cry, "Hew, fight, smite, break, shove, knock, smash, and crash the idols. If you see a crucifix, spit in its face." The people are stirred up to violence whereas judgment has been committed to the civil magistrates. I had not said that Carlstadt is a murderous prophet, but I do say that he has a rebellious, murderous, and sectarian spirit which will break out, given the chance. We are under princes. We must wait for them and if they do nothing we can put the images out of our hearts.

This is not to say that I am defending images, but since they are an outward thing I will not let the murderous spirits burden consciences with a new law. As I said above, the law of Moses, strictly interpreted, does not forbid crucifixes nor images of the saints, which as a matter of fact are useful and commendable, as a remembrance and a sign. In any case only that portion of the Ten Commandments is now binding which enshrines the natural law: "Thou shalt not steal. Thou shalt not kill. Thou shalt not commit adultery," etc. But not the injunction as to the Sabbath. If Carlstadt keeps on, he will have us observing Sunday on Saturday. These image smashers read my German Bible which is full of pictures, and if they are not objectionable in the book, why should they be on a wall? When I think of the passion of Christ I have to picture it and if I may do so without sin in my heart why not before my eye? But I am afraid by this argument I may persuade the image breakers not to read my Bible.

When I went down to Orlamünde [*Carlstadt's parish*] I found that he had started up insurrection and sectarianism. I am glad that he has been banished and I do not want him back unless he becomes a different Andreas. He says he will not murder but I do not trust him. After he has announced the command of Moses to exterminate the ungodly to the people, how will we hold them back? You cannot trifle with the mob. You say, "Let him talk. Dissuade him." Whom? Carlstadt? *Ja wohl!* When did he ever listen to us? He calls us twice-Papists and cousins of Antichrist.

The land belongs to the princes of Saxony and not to Carlstadt who is a guest. If they don't want him they don't have to tell why. Does an innkeeper have to tell why he throws out a guest? In that case, he would be a captive.

As for the Mass, where has Christ forbidden elevation? The Pope transgresses when he commands it and the sectaries when they forbid it. Chasubles and albs should be free. We do not have to do exactly what Christ did, otherwise we should have to walk on water. Even the Papists do not claim that when they elevate the host they are making a sacrifice, but Carlstadt always plays on the same fiddle and looks at the outward.

They're always talking about "spirit, spirit" and that everything must be inward. They say: "Can a handful of water wash away my sins? Can bread and wine help me? No, No! I must eat the flesh of Christ spiritually." "The Wittenbergers," they say, "have stolen faith out of the letter." One would think that those who so speak were possessed of five Holy Ghosts. If you ask them how one gets this high spirit they point not to the outward Gospel, but to the land of dreams. "Stand in stillness, like me," they say, "and heavenly voices will come to you. God himself will talk with you." But they don't tell you how the spirit comes to you nor how you get to the spirit so that you can travel on the clouds and ride on the wind. They don't tell you how, or when, or what, but only that you will have to find out for yourself, the way they have done. They establish outwardly what God has neither ordered nor forbidden, but they forbid images, churches, and altars. They will not speak of the Mass or sacrifice or elevation. They wear no chasuble but only a grey cloak. They reject all titles save that of "dear neighbor." They would kill a godless priest and are unwilling to suffer beneath injustice. He who does not agree with them is a double-Papist, a scribe, and a murderer of Christ.

Carlstadt says that Christ's body cannot be in the Sacrament because Carlstadt cannot conceive how the body that hung on the cross could be in the elements. To be sure the most feeble reason would prefer to say that simply bread and wine are there. No special spirit is necessary to make one feel in that way. I should find it easy, but if we are going to inject our murky understanding into the Scripture not a particle of faith will remain. I would have to say, "I cannot believe that God's Son became a man, that the majesty which heaven and earth cannot comprise was contained in the womb of a woman and crucified upon a cross." Our principle is this, when the Holy Scripture gives something to be believed, we should not diverge from the words as they are unless some article of the faith requires us to interpret them other than as they sound. As for example, when the Bible says, "God is my rock," this must be figurative because He is not an ordinary stone. But there is no article of faith which requires us to interpret, "This is my body," figuratively. Paul says, "The cup of blessing which we bless, is it not the communion of the blood of Christ? The bread which we break, is it not the communion of the body of Christ?" [*I Corinthians 10:16.*] This is the thunder-ax that chops off the head of Carlstadt and all the sectaries. He says this passage refers to spiritual communion. Again you see how this slippery devil makes spiritual what God has made physical. Carlstadt even misrepresents the Papists. The pope does not say to the bread, "My God, have mercy on me." The pope does not teach that one should think of the bread and forget Christ. The pope does not hold that our sins are forgiven through the bread.

I warn Carlstadt that he must repent. God has been tried long enough and will not be patient forever. God grant that I am here a liar and a false prophet. I will say no more. Though Christ were crucified for us a thousand times, it would do us no good unless the Word of God came to bring this message to us, saying, "This is yours, take it and have it for your own."

## VI. Carlstadt: *On the Old and the New Covenants. How Carlstadt Recanted*, March 16, 1525

The Evangelists Matthew and Luke relate that Christ took the cup and gave to His disciples saying, "Drink all of you of it." And then afterwards he said, "This is my blood of the new covenant which is shed for you and for many for the remission of sins." [*Matthew 26; Mark 14.*] From this we see that the disciples drank ordinary wine because the Papists teach that the bread and the wine remain unchanged prior to the words of consecration. Therefore, the disciples drank wine before it was turned into blood and we cannot conclude that at the First Lord's Supper the disciples drank physically the blood of the Lord. Some of the priests make Christ say, "Let all of you drink of this blood," but you laymen who have searched the Scriptures for yourselves, will see the truth. Luther does not rely on Matthew and Mark, rather on Luke and Paul. [*Luke 22; First Corinthians 11.*] He takes the Lukan form "this cup is the new covenant in my blood" [*Luke 22:20*] and says that the cup must have contained blood. This he says is the thunder-ax that chops off Carlstadt's head. Thus the new Pope keeps the words of the old Pope. But the blood of Christ shed upon the cross, if it is to be a new covenant, must be a spiritual sprinkling and a forgiveness of sins. There are two characteristics of the new covenant: That the law of God is inscribed in the heart and that sins are forgiven. [*Jeremiah 31; Isaiah 43.*] Christ as a spiritual priest through the Holy Spirit pours His blood into the heart, soul, and conscience and cleanses our hearts, and consciences through faith. I ask only to be taught by clear, unmistakable, and certain testimony of Scripture. What shall I do when I am struck with a thunder-ax and consigned to the devil?

# — Reading No. 5 —

# THE REFORMED CHURCHES: ZWINGLI AND THE ANABAPTISTS[5]

*The* Sixty-Seven Articles *of Zwingli provide an admirable summary of his proposed reforms and highlight the differences with Luther as to the doctrine of the Lord's Supper and the attitude to fasts, feasts, vestments, and the like. These articles served as the basis for the first Zürich disputation. The articles in full and the acts of the disputation are translated in* Selected Works of Huldreich

[5]  I. *"Huldreich Zwinglis sämmtliche Werke"* I, *Corpus Reformatorum* LXXXVIII.

   II. *The Latin Works of Huldreich Zwingli,* ed. Clarence N. Heller (Philadelphia, 1929), III, pp. 184-96.

   III. *The Latin Works of Huldreich Zwingli,* ed. William John Henke (Philadelphia, 1922), II, p. 194.

   IV. *Ibid.,* pp. 198-99, 205, 209, 211-15.

   V. *Ibid.,* pp. 199-200, 229.

   VI. Translated by John C. Wenger, *Mennonite Quarterly Review,* XX, 4 (October, 1948), pp. 243-54.

   VII. Henry C. Vedder, *Balthasar Hübmaier* (New York, 1905), p. 213.

   VIII. *"Quellen und Geschichte der Wiedertäufer"* II (Leipzig, 1934), ed. Karl Schornbaum in *Quellen und Forschungen zur Reformationsgeschichte* XVI, p. 84.

   IX. Lydia Müller, *"Glaubenszeugnisse oberdeutscher Taufgesinnten,"* in *Quellen und Forschungen zur Reformationsgeschichte* XX (Leipzig, 1938), pp. 199, 249, and *Die älteste Chronik der Hutterischen Brüder,* ed. A. J. F. Ziegelschmid (Ithaca, New York), 1943, p. 307.

   X. *Ibid.,* pp. 285, 288, 293.

   XI. Passages culled by John Horsch from *The Complete Works of Menno Simons* (Elkart, Indians, 1871) and included in his *Menno Simons* (Scotsdale, Pa., 1916), pp. 256-93.

Zwingli, *edited by Samuel Macauley Jackson (Phila-delphia, 1901), pp. 40-117.*

*The four selections which follow from Zwingli are from two works arranged topically so that each work is listed twice. They illustrate first his denuding the sacraments of genuinely sacramental import. He calls the Lord's Supper the Eucharist, a word derived from the Greek meaning* thanksgiving *and applied in the early church to the Supper. Note in the final section that the mark of election is faith.*

*The selections from the Anabaptists have been chosen to illustrate the main tenets and to represent the main groups. The doctrines covered are these: the ethical demands, discipline through the ban, the doctrine of the Lord's Supper and baptism, including the rejection of infant baptism, the practice of communism, the rejection of war and the very qualified endorsement of government, the rejection of constraint in religion. The groups represented are the Swiss, the Mennonites in Holland, and the Hutterites in Moravia.*

✓          ✓          ✓

I. Zwingli's Sixty-Seven Articles Presented at the First Zürich Disputation, January 19, 1523

1. Those who say that the Gospel is nothing without the confirmation of the Church err and blaspheme God.

2. The sum of the Gospel is that our Lord, Jesus Christ, God's dear Son, has revealed to us the will of His Father and by His innocence has redeemed us from death and has reconciled God.

7. He is the salvation and head of all believers who are his body.

8. Hence, all those who live in this head are members and sons of God, and this is the Church, the communion of the saints, the bride of Christ, the Catholic Church.

9. Consequently the so-called ecclesiastical pomp, holy days, estates, titles and laws are sheer foolishness because they do not agree with Christ, the Head.

13. One who is redeemed by him learns clearly and purely the Word of God and by his spirit is drawn to him and transformed into him.

17. On the Pope: Christ is the one eternal high priest,

therefore those who vaunt themselves as high priests oppose the honor and power of Christ.

18. On the Mass: Christ who gave himself once and for all upon the cross is a sacrifice and victim making satisfaction in eternity for the sins of all the faithful. Hence the Mass is not a sacrifice, but a commemoration of the sacrifice made once and for all upon the cross and is, as it were, a sign of our redemption in Christ.

19. On the intercession of the saints: Christ is the only mediator.

20. God gives us everything in the name of Christ. Hence we need no other intercessors.

22. Of good works: Since Christ is our righteousness, our works are good only insofar as they are of Christ.

24. On dietary laws and clothes: Since a Christian is not bound to works which God has not enjoined, any food may be eaten at any time and special permits to eat cheese and butter are an imposture.

26. God's disapproval of hypocrisy does away with cowls, vestments, and tonsures.

29. On clerical marriage: The clergy sin, if discovering that God has denied them the gift of chastity, they do not marry.

31. On the ban: No private individual can impose the ban, but only the Church in conjunction with the minister.

33. On unjust gain: Unjust gains, if they cannot be duly restored, should not be given to temples, cloisters, monks, priests, and nuns but to the needy.

36. The temporal authority arrogated by priests belongs to the civil government.

37. Whom all Christians are obligated to obey.

38. Provided they do nothing against God.

40. Magistrates may take the lives of those guilty of public offense.

42. If magistrates go against the rule of Christ they may be deposed.

43. That kingdom is best and soundest which is from God and in God.

44. Concerning prayers: Since the true worshippers worship God in spirit and in truth.

46. Singing or rather bawling in churches without piety and for gain is done simply to be seen and recompensed by men.

49. Concerning offense: There is no greater offense than that marriage should be forbidden to priests but they are allowed to have concubines or harlots and are taxed on this account.

51. Absolution: to attribute absolution to a creature is to deprive God of His glory.

52. Consequently, confession to a priest or a neighbor is not for remission of sins but for counseling.

53. Works of satisfaction imposed by a priest are a human device, except excommunication.

54. To ascribe to works of satisfaction what Christ has done is to condemn God.

55. He who declines to remit any sin to a penitent stands not in the place of God or Peter but of the devil.

56. He who remits any sin for money is a confederate of Simon Magus and Baalam and a legate of the devil.

57. On purgatory: Scripture knows of no purgatory beyond this life.

58. The judgment of the dead is known only to God.

61. On the priesthood: With regard to the [indelible] character of the priest, lately claimed, Scripture knows nothing.

64. On the reform of abuse: Those who confess their errors may be left to die in peace and thereafter their revenues may be redistributed.

65. Those who do not, are not to be molested with violence unless they so carry themselves that the magistrates must step in for the public peace.

66. Let the clergy erect the cross of Christ and not money boxes. The ax is laid to the root of the tree.

67. I am willing to discuss tithes, infant baptism, and confirmation.

## II. Huldreich Zwingli: *On True and False Religion,* March, 1525

The *sacraments* are signs or ceremonials by which a man proves to the Church that he either aims to be or is a soldier of Christ and which inform the whole Church rather than yourselves of your faith, for if your faith is not so perfect as not to need a ceremonial sign it is not faith.

*Baptism* is an initiatory sacrament by which those who were going to change their life and ways marked themselves out and were enrolled among the repentant. How the baptism of John and Christ differed is an unprofitable question, for there is really no difference at all as far as the reason and purpose are concerned. John's dipping effected nothing—I'm speaking here of the baptism of water not of the inward flooding wrought through the Holy Spirit. Christ's dipping effects nothing; for Christ was satisfied with the baptism of John. (*The disciples*) were baptized with no baptism but that of John, for Christ baptized not. To baptize into the name of the Father and the Son, etc. is in reality nothing else than to dedicate, devote and consecrate those who were previously of the world and the flesh to the Father, Son and Holy Spirit. But it is a mere outward thing, this dipping to the accompaniment of the sacred words "in the name of the Father and of the Son and of the Holy Ghost"— a sign and ceremony signifying the real thing.

### III. *On the Providence of God,* August 20, 1530

*Infant Baptism:* Baptism is not given to anyone unless he first confesses that he has faith, if he is a grown person or unless he has the promise in virtue of which he is counted a member of the Church, if he is a child. The promise is that the Gentiles, when they have obtained the knowledge of God, and true religion, shall be just as much of the Church and people of God as the Hebrews. Since, therefore, the children of the Hebrews have always been counted with the Church with their parents, and the divine promise is sure, it is clear that the children of Christians belong to the Church as much as their parents. This promise is not conveyed in baptism but he to whom it has previously been given is baptized that by a visible sign he may bear witness that he is of the number of those who are called the people of God. Here surely nothing is brought in, but that which has previously been given is recognized by a religious rite.

### IV. *On True and False Religion,* March, 1525

The *Eucharist:* I fear that if there is anywhere pernicious error in the adoration and worship of the one true God, it is in the abuse of the Eucharist. Now we are all bent upon handling holy things rather than upon making ourselves holy. The result is that we worship with embraces and kisses wood, stone, earth, dust, shoes, vestments, rings, hats, swords, belts, bones, teeth, hair, milk, bread, tablets, wine, knives, jars and anything that pious men have ever handled. When Christ said, "The bread which I am about to give to you is my flesh," he was not talking of sacramental eating but of the eating of faith. The flesh of Christ profiteth not by being eaten, but by being slain. I unwaveringly believe that there is one and only one way to heaven, firmly to believe and trust in the Son of God and to ascribe no power to any of the elements of this world, that is the things of sense, and those who say, "You seem to me to hold that the bodily flesh and also the blood of Christ are not present in the Eucharist," I answer, "The flesh profiteth nothing." Faith exists in our hearts by the spirit of God and we are sensible of it. That there is an inward change of heart is not an obscure matter but we do not come to it by means of the senses.

## V. *On the Providence of God,* August 20, 1530

*Election:* Faith is given to the elect only. Election therefore precedes faith. Hence those who have been elected and do not come to a knowledge of faith, like infants, attain everlasting happiness nonetheless. We do not know about the election of any. It is not, therefore, a universal rule that he who has not faith is damned, but he who has heard the doctrine of faith expounded and remains and dies in unbelief can perhaps be accounted among the wretched. Therefore, when the gaining of eternal salvation is attributed to faith that is attributed to the secondary faith, to the seal as it were, which belongs to the primary and the instrument, faith is the sign of the election by which we obtain true blessedness. . . . If poverty, illness, childlessness, slighting and defeat are our portion and we attribute them to Providence, what comfort we receive in such adversity! With what high spirit think you such a man rises above the world and scorns what is below him! Having said to himself, "These things are given me by Divine Providence." The cup must be drained therefore and the battle won by endurance with undaunted soul. You are God's tool. He wills to wear you out by use not by idleness. Oh happy man, whom He calls to His work!

## VI. The Anabaptists: The Swiss Brethren *On Christian Morality and Discipline,* Anonymous, Before 1530

When Paul says in Romans 3 that those who are justified in Christ are justified without any merit or without the works of the Law, he does not mean that a man can be saved without the works of faith. How did Christ make satisfaction for our sins? Answer: He made satisfaction not only for ourselves but for the sins of the whole world insofar as men believe on him and follow him according to the demands of faith. Blessed is the man who keeps the middle way, not yielding to the work-saints, who promise salvation or the forgiveness of sins through works apart from faith—all their works are like wild plums—nor to the scribes who veer to the right and under the name of the Gospel teach a faith without works, taking the poor and obedient Christ as their satisfaction though they do not wish to hear what he says. They wish to obey God only with the soul and not with the body in order that they may escape persecution. They think that faith is a false and empty delusion. That is why they can say that infants have faith though they give no evidence in works even after they are grown. How well can one see here the beast with the seven heads and the ten horns!

## VII. Balthasar Hübmaier: *Concerning the Christian Ban*

The ban is exclusion and separation to such an extent that no fellowship is held with an excommunicated person by ·Christians whether in speaking, eating, drinking, grinding, baking or in any other way, but he is treated as a heathen and a publican, that is as an offensive, disorderly and venomous man who is bound and delivered over to Satan. He is to be avoided and shunned.

## VIII. Answers of Imprisoned Anabaptists in 1528

*The Lord's Supper:* The flesh and blood of Christ are not changed into bread. The bread which he brake is the Gospel. If it had not been broken, it would not have gone into all the world. When one has the Word and seals it in the heart, as Christ taught, this is to partake of the body of Christ in the spirit. And the cup which Christ gave to his disciples means his suffering. The blood in the cup means the blood of Christ in the bodies of men. When a man is a Christian, he has the blood of Christ, and if suffering comes, that is the cup in the blood.

## IX. Confession of the Brethren Arrested at Trieste, 1539, and *The Five Articles,* Possibly by Hans Denk in 1526, and *The Five Articles* of 1547

*Government:* Further with regard to the sword it was asked whether a Christian could be a magistrate if he were chosen. To this we replied, "Christ was invited to be a king, but he fled. We follow him in this for the kingdom of Christ is not of this world. Moreover he forbade the power of the sword and said, 'The rulers of the Gentiles lord it over them,' and the rulers use force, but 'it shall not be so among you.' " Further it was asked whether a Christian could be a judge in disputes among unbelievers. To this we confess and testify that Christ declined to judge of the inheritance. Again we affirm that a Christian man may not be a magistrate. Why? Because the government of the world is of the flesh and that of the Christian according to the spirit. The citizenship of the world is in the world, but the Christian citizenship is in heaven. . . .

Christ said, "Behold I send you forth as sheep among wolves." A sheep is a defenseless, patient beast equipped with no means of defense save to flee as far as he can and may. The way of the Christian is as little compatible with the government of the sword as is the sheep with the wolf or the lion. . . .

Our will and mind are not, however, to do away with worldly government or not to be obedient to it in goods and sanctions because a government shall and must be in the world, just as a schoolmaster must have rods among children. Therefore, the magistrate is ordained of God.

## X. The Hutterian Brethren: *The Five Articles* of 1547

*Community of Goods:* Now that God has brought the Christian Church up out of Egypt, as they pass through the wilderness of this world, the rich should not have more than the poor nor the poor than the rich. One of the chief articles of the creed is to believe in the com-

munion of the saints. This means not only in things
spiritual but also in things temporal. In the Book of
Acts we read that the believers in Jerusalem numbered
five thousand and that they had all things in common.

## XI. The Teachings of Menno Simons
### (1496-1561) in Holland

Before God neither baptism nor the Supper nor any
other outward ordinances avail if partaken without the
spirit of God and a new creature. We are not regenerated
because we have been baptized. We are baptized because
we have been regenerated by faith and the Word of God.
Faith is to precede baptism. Since we do not find in
Scripture a single word by which Christ has ordained the
baptism of infants or that his apostles taught and practiced it, we say and confess rightly that infant baptism
is but a human invention. Even if there were a sleeping
faith in unconscious infants, they should not be baptized
before they can verbally confess it. But although infants
have neither faith nor baptism, think not that they are
lost. Oh no, they are saved because they have the Lord's
own promise of the Kingdom of God.

We confess the Lord's Supper to be a sacramental sign
instituted by the Lord himself with bread and wine to
remind us that he has offered his holy body and shed
his precious blood for the remissions of our sins. Consequently, it is an emblem of Christian love, unity and
peace in the Church of Christ, and thirdly a communion
of the body and blood of Christ which means that Christ
in his great love has accepted us and we have become
partakers of him. A third ordinance [after baptism and
the Lord's Supper] is the washing of the feet of the saints
which Jesus instituted to show that he must cleanse us
according to the inner man and we should humble ourselves for one another.

The regenerated do not go to war nor fight. They are
the children of peace who have broken their swords into
plowshares. Spears and swords of iron we leave to those
who, alas, consider human blood and swines' blood of
well nigh equal value. The truly baptized disciples of
Christ, baptized inwardly with the spirit and with fire and
outwardly with water, know of no weapons save patience,
hope, non-resistance, and God's Word. The authorities

say that it is right to swear if it be to the truth. Christ
said, "Swear not at all." Rulers are to be obeyed when
their commands are not contrary to God's Word as in
such lawful matters as working on dykes, roads, rivers,
paying duty, taxes, tribute, etc. But if rulers lord it over
consciences we do not consent. We would rather give up
all we own and suffer slander, scourging, persecution,
anxiety, famine, thirst, nakedness, cold, heat, poverty,
imprisonment, banishment, fire and sword than forsake
the truth of God or depart from the love of Christ. Faith
is a gift of God and cannot be forced by the sword nor
is it the will of the Master that the tares should be rooted
up before the day of the harvest. Where did the Holy
Scriptures teach that in Christ's kingdom the Church,
conscience, and faith should be ruled by the sword of
the magistrate?

— Reading No. 6 —

# THE REFORMED CHURCHES: CALVINISM[6]

*The thought of John Calvin is commonly illustrated
from his great work* The Institutes of the Christian Religion. *It is a great work and a wonderfully systematic*

[6] The documents in this reading are taken from (I) *Calvini
Opera, Corpus Reformatorum*, XXXV, pp. 21-22, 77-80,
167-69, 99, 106, 56; (II) *Ibid.*, I; (III) *Calvini Opera*, ed.
Niesel and Barth (1926), I, p. 423; (IV) *Ibid.*, p. 250; (V)
a. *Calvini Opera, Corpus Reformatorum*, XLV, p. 172; b.
*Ibid.*, II, pp. 666-67, *Institutes* III, 20, 42; (VI) a. *Ibid.*,
XIII, p. 81, Ep. 1085; b. *Ibid.*, XVII, pp. 673-74. Ep. 3133;
c. *Ibid.*, XVIII, pp. 425-26. Ep. 3174; d. *Ibid.*, XX, p. 244
f., Ep. 4074.

*presentation of his teachings It figures little in the follow-
ing selections partly because it is so readily available in
English translation, partly because the temper of Calvinism is better disclosed in some of the Biblical commentaries and the letters. There one discovers that Calvin
was far from a cool and dispassionate theologian. His
words pulsate with indignation, reproof, exhortation, and
exaltation. The* Sermons of Deuteronomy *give a better
notion than do the* Institutes *of how he felt with regard to God's sovereignty. The preface to the* Institutes
*is a letter and rings with indignation and lofty admonition
to the very king of France. This preface and the letters
illustrate the Calvinist technique of seeking to enlist key
figures in the political world. Calvin's views on election,
the kingdom of God and the Church are of extreme importance if one would understand the impact of Calvinism on the social order.*

✓          ✓          ✓

I. Calvin on the Sovereignty of God
—From the *Sermons on Deuteronomy,* 1555

Observe in connection with the deliverance of the Is-
raelites that the main point is not that God should save
us from the hands of our enemies and keep us longer in
this world. What good were all that, if God were not
gracious to us and if we did not call upon Him and
commit ourselves to Him? There is no point in our staying
here three days and a half, for what is this life if not
a feeble shadow which passes soon away? The point is
rather that we should recognize God as our eternal
Saviour, that we so walk in His fear that we may expect
from Him not only guidance for a brief moment but
that in the end He should take us to Himself, that
after this pilgrimage we may enjoy an inheritance laid
up for us in heaven. The blessings of this life are to be
used only for our salvation, otherwise they become a
curse and those on whom God has conferred the most
are the most blameworthy in His eyes, for we corrupt all
the graces of God when we are not incited by them to
render Him homage, placing ourselves completely in His
hands as our refuge. Let us then not be as the brute
beasts grubbing in the earth, but let us lift our eyes to
the heavens and recognize that He calls us to Himself

and that toward Him we move till we be conjoined with Him forever.

All our prayers must be brought into conformity with God's will. If in excess of fervor we ask for something not duly considered, then we should add "nevertheless Thy will be done." A man, for example, with a sick child or wife may cry out in vehement affection, "O my God, wilt Thou not have pity upon me? Must I be afflicted to the very end?" Such a prayer is at fault and should be corrected by adding "O my God, this is indeed my wish and Thou knowest full well the reason, yet I must render unto Thee that which Thou hast placed above all else, obedience. O Lord dispose of me and all that is mine according to Thy will." When God afflicts us we are not to try to escape from His hand. Follow rather the example of Moses. He was himself deprived of the heritage promised to his people. God had made him a leader but now, just before his death, he found himself demoted, branded with ignominy, denied entrance to the Land of Promise. Among the six thousand persons who came up out of Egypt there was not one more deserving than he to enter. He might well have been disgruntled and have said, "What trials I have had to lead this people! God has worked miracles by my hand and even now I have such zeal for His honor and the salvation of this people that I never weary in this cause. Am I then to be excluded and others go in who have not done a mite of what I have contributed?" Moses might thus have chafed and might have said further, "Very well, God is through with me. All right, I am through with Him. I will quit. Let Him get somebody else." But no, although God had humiliated him before men, denying him that for which he most longed and suffering others to go on ahead, yet Moses said, "My friends, even though I die here I will not cease to do my duty." He might have blamed the people who had provoked the offense for which he lost the earthly inheritance, but he said merely, "God has sworn that I shall not pass over Jordan unto the Promised Land." No murmurs and no blasphemies passed his lips, but he crucified himself.

Oh you people of Geneva, be not like young bulls who will not bear the yoke, for God has created you to this end that you should serve and honor Him from the womb of your mothers and be wholly devoted to Him. And now see the Christianity of this Geneva, where the Gospel has been preached these twenty years, so that the very walls should resound with it and the sidewalks show some mark of the truth of God. And yet, these enraged beasts are as rude in their rebellion as horned bulls. Listen to God who says to you, "It is true that you are weak and that you have a mighty enemy. You are not able to resist unless you are strengthened and aided by Me, but I assure you that your temptations will not exceed your power. I know what you can do, and I will give you the strength needed. Though the world and the devil rage against you, I will curb them all. However you are assailed, you will come through. Hold to that." Has God really spoken like this? Doubt it not. Of course, this does not mean that we can be entirely delivered from fear while we are on earth, but look not to the dangers by which we are beset. This fear must not so lay hold of us that we fail to take courage and call upon God, to rest in Him and go foward.

## II. Preface to the *Institutes of the Christian Religion* Addressed to Francis I of France, 1536

To the most puissant, illustrious monarch, Francis most Christian King of France, John Calvin wishes peace and salvation in the Lord. I have resolved to present to you a confession that you may learn what is that doctrine against which the furious so rage who disturb thy kingdom with fire and sword. Daily this teaching is traduced before the most noble king as designed to wrest scepters from kings, overthrow judicial procedures, subvert all order and government, disturb the tranquillity of the people, abrogate laws, dissipate possessions and introduce sheer chaos. Wherefore, most invincible King, not without reason do I request that you assume full cognizance of this cause. Be not deterred out of contempt for our lowliness. Though we be but the offscouring of the earth, yet our doctrine is sublime above all the glory of the world and must stand, because it is not ours but the doctrine of the living God and His Christ. This teaching is calumniated as new, unconfirmed by miracles and refuted by its fruits which are sects, seditions, and sins. Opponents call it new because Christ and the Gospel are new to them and that is why they think it uncertain. As for miracles there is no need of any more because we teach no recent Gospel but that Gospel which was long ago confirmed by the miracles of Christ and the apostles. Most magnanimous King, listen not to the groundless delations by which our adversaries seek to alarm you, charging that our new Gospel, as they call it, has no other intent but to seek opportunity for sedition and impunity for vice. We who are thus accused of meditating the subversion of kingdoms have never uttered a factious word. As for our deportment, although there may be something to reprove, yet there is nothing worthy of such insult. Most glorious King, though now your mind may be averse, alienated and even inflamed against us, we hope to regain your favor, if your Majesty will but once read this our confession with composure. If on the contrary, your ears are lent to the malevolent and no defense is permitted to the accused, if we then continue to be persecuted, with connivance on your part, by imprisonment, scourges, tortures, confiscations and flames, then like sheep for the slaughter, reduced to extremities we will in patience possess our souls and await the mighty hand of the Lord who will undoubtedly come in due time to deliver the poor from their affliction and to castigate those who swagger in their security. May the King of kings establish your throne in righteousness and your kingdom in equity, most mighty and illustrious King. From Basel on the Calends of August 1536.

### III. *The Genevan Confession* of 1537

*Article 16.* The Supper of our Lord is a sign by which under the bread and the wine He represents the true spiritual communication which we have in His body and blood. According to his ordinance it should be distributed among the company of the faithful that those who wish to have Jesus for their life may participate and because the Mass of the Pope has been an accursed and diabolical ordinance to overthrow the mystery of the Holy Supper, we declare that we hold it in execration as an idolatry condemned by God because it is regarded as a sacrifice for redemption of souls and because the bread is adored as God.

IV. Interchange of Calvin and Cardinal Sadoleto

Sadoleto, the Catholic bishop of the district of Geneva sought to recall his Calvinist parishioners to the Catholic faith, first by reminding them that the chief end of man is his own salvation. "There is a better chance of security," said he, "in the Church tradition of fifteen hundred or at least thirteen hundred years than among innovators with only twenty-five years standing. A Catholic who at the Judgment Day declares his fidelity to the ancient faith, even though he be wrong, which God forbid, will stand a better chance because of sincerity, humility and obedience than will an arrogant innovator."

Calvin replied, "I cannot understand why you have addressed to us such a long exordium on the importance of the future life with which we are continually preoccupied, but I will say that it is unworthy of a theologian to permit man to be so concerned about himself and not rather to make zeal for God's glory the chief object of his life. I confess that God, in order to make the glory of His name more congenial to men, has conjoined our salvation with zeal for its promotion and extension. Nevertheless, the Christian man should aspire to a loftier goal than the salvation of his soul. No one imbued with true piety will consider your appeal for concern with the future life because it directs a man wholly to himself and not with a single word lifts him up to hallow the name of God.

V. Calvin on the Kingdom of God and the Church

A. From the *Commentary on the Harmony of the Gospels,* 1555. The kingdom of heaven is taken to mean the renovation of the Church, as now it has already been arising through the preaching of the Gospel.

B. From *The Institutes of the Christian Religion,* 1559. (*Commenting on the verse in the Lord's Prayer, "Thy kingdom."*) Although I have previously defined God's kingdom, I will briefly repeat. God reigns where men in self denial and contempt of the world and of the life terrestrial dedicate themselves to God and aspire to the life celestial.

God erects his kingdom by humbling the whole world, but in different ways. He masters the lasciviousness of some and breaks the indomitable pride of others. Daily it is to be desired that God should gather the churches to Himself from amid the ills of the world; that he should extend and increase the churches, enrich them with his gifts, establish in them a legitimate order, conversely, that he should vanquish all enemies of the pure doctrine and religion, dissipate their councils, and frustrate their endeavors. Wherefore, not in vain do we strive for daily progress because the affairs of men never so thrive as when vices are purged and integrity flourishes. The fullness of progress is projected until the final coming of Christ when as Paul says "God will be all in all." (*I Corinthians 15:28.*) Therefore this prayer should restrain us from the corruptions of the world which separate us from God and prevent His kingdom from flourishing among us. At the same time our zeal should be kindled for the mortification of the flesh and even the bearing of the cross because in this way God wishes to advance His kingdom. It matters not if the outward man perishes so long as the inward is renewed. This is the condition of God's kingdom that while we submit to His justice He makes us partners in His glory.

As for the visible Church the Scriptures speak of it in two ways. Sometimes they mean the Church which is truly in the presence of God in which none are received save those who by the grace of adoption are the sons of God and by the spirit of sanctification are true members of Christ. This means not only the saints on earth, but also the elect from the foundation of the world. But often the word church is applied to the entire multitude of men gathered throughout the world who profess to worship one God in Christ, have been initiated into His faith by baptism, and by participation in the Lord's Supper testify to unity in doctrine and charity. They consent to the Word of God and uphold the ministry instituted by Christ for the preaching of the Word. In this church many hypocrites are mixed who have nothing of Christ but the title and appearance. Many are ambitious, avaricious, envious, slanderous. Some are impure. For the time they are tolerated, either because they can be convicted by no legitimate judgment or because discipline is not adequately severe. But although we should ever believe in the Church to us invisible and known only to the eyes of God, yet we should have regard unto that which is called the Church with respect to men and we should cherish her communion.

Moreover, since it is desirable that we should be able to recognize her, God has appointed certain marks and as it were symbols, for it is the singular prerogative of God to know His own. Lest we be too presumptuous we are daily admonished by examples of how far His secret judgments exceed our comprehension. For those who seem to us utterly abandoned are recalled by His goodness, and those who appear to others to stand often fall. As Augustine says in accord with the hidden predestination of God, there are many sheep without and many wolves within. But that we might know approximately those who are to be regarded by us as God's sons, He has accommodated Himself in a measure to our understanding. Since the certitude of faith was not necessary, He has substituted for it the judgment of charity whereby we recognize as members of the Church those who make profession with us of the same God and Christ by confession of faith, example of life, and participation in the sacraments.

## VI. Letters of Calvin

A. *To the Duke of Somerset, October 1548.* That I may address myself more particularly to you, most noble lord, I hear that there are two kinds of subversives [*in England*] who connive against the king and the head of the realm. There are first demented folk who in the name of the Gospel stir up disorder and secondly those who are hardened in the superstitions of Anti-Christ. Both deserve to be coerced by the avenging sword which the Lord has committed to you because they rise up not only against the king but against God Himself, who has set the king upon his throne and installed you as Protector not only of his person but also of his kingly majesty.

B. *To John Tarnow in Cracow, March 1554.* Most generous and illustrious Prince, since I learn from your letters that my correspondence pleases you, I am emboldened to admonish you the more. Everything hinges on this, that you do not deem it discreet to purge the Church of Poland of the uncleanness of the Papacy.

I am not prepared to concede that the peace of your kingdom has been disturbed by our actions. You write a hard word when you say that many commotions within and without have been occasioned by religion, for even if perverseness and ambition have incited some and contumacy and impiety have impelled others to conflict, nevertheless the blame is not properly to be cast upon the heavenly doctrine. God will not leave unpunished such an indignity as to make Him the author of discord at the very moment when He is seeking to reconcile men to mutual concord. The sincere worship of God and His holy truth, in which repose our eternal salvation should mean more to us than a hundred worlds.

C. *To Admiral Coligny, April 1561.* My dear sir, I have been informed by my brother that you would like from me a disclaimer of the conspiracy of Amboise. I would have done so long ago had I considered only myself, but I feared that I should seem to gloat over the calamity of those poor fellows whose only crime was an excess of zeal. Yet, I have not concealed my disapproval. Some seven or eight months ago someone in charge of a company asked me whether it is proper to resist the tyranny by which the children of God are oppressed and by what means. I tried to show him that there is no warrant from God and that even from the standpoint of the world rebellion is presumption and will have no good issue. He replied with some heat that it was not a question of attacking the king or his authority but of requiring the enforcement of the laws of the country in view of the king's minority. There was a constant fear, said he, that a frightful massacre would wipe out the faithful. I replied simply that if a drop of blood were shed, the rivers of all Europe would run red. Better that we should all perish one hundred times than that the cause of the Gospel and Christianity should be exposed to such opprobrium.

D. *To Renée the Duchess of Ferrara, January 1564. Renée had complained of the way in which the ministers spoke of her son-in-law, the Duke of Guise. Calvin replied.*

Madame, I learned from your last letter that you wished me to reprove certain ministers for harsh judgments on the late Duke of Guise. I perceive that affection causes you to forget what would otherwise well be recognized. I reminded you before that David used to hate God's enemies. You reply that this was under the old dispensation of the law. Madame, such a gloss would overthrow all Scripture. David returned good for evil but when he hated the reprobate there is no doubt that he was actuated by a pure zeal. He was a type of our Saviour, Jesus Christ, and if we pretend to exceed in humanity him who was the fountain of mercy, woe to us.

Madame, you are not alone in suffering bitter anguish over the horrors of these days, although it touches you more closely because of the crown from which you are sprung. Monsieur de Guise lit the fire and he cannot be spared. Although I have prayed that God would grant him mercy, I have often wished that God would lay His hand upon him and deliver the Church, provided he were not converted. I can say that before the war it was entirely due to me that he was not assassinated. To damn him is too much. Unless one has an infallible mark of his reprobation, we must beware of presumption, because there is only one Judge before whom we must all answer. As for assigning the King of Navarre to heaven and the Duke of Guise to hell that is too much. Nevertheless, Madame, although we may pray for the salvation of anyone, this is not to commend him as if he were a member of the Church. If we ask God to stay those who are on the way to perdition, that does not mean that we regard them as brothers and desire their general prosperity. When the King of Navarre was guilty of defection and his minister stopped praying for him, the Queen of Navarre remonstrated. The minister replied that he could do no more than pray for his conversion. The Queen acquiesced. Now, the King was closer to her than your son-in-law is to you. Nevertheless, she conquered her affection rather than that the name of God should be profaned. I ask you in the name of charity whether attachment to one man should outweigh concern for one hundred thousand? The cure is to hate evil without attaching it to persons and leave each to his Judge.

# THE ANGLICAN CHURCH ESTABLISHED[7]

*One observes that all of the selections in this reading are from public documents. Even the* Book of Common Prayer *was promulgated by the crown. This is not to say that the English Reformation produced no theological literature. The publications of the Parker Society witness to the contrary. Nevertheless England in this period produced no reformer of the stature of Luther, Zwingli, or Calvin. The Archbishop of Canterbury, Thomas Cranmer, is distinguished primarily because of the* Book of Common Prayer.

*The documents selected for Henry VIII show the beginnings of the breach with Rome. For the later acts see the work by Gee and Hardy listed below in the note. For Edward VI the excerpts are from the* Book of Common Prayer. *Its magnificent diction and sonorous cadences make of it a monument of literature as well as of religion. The expression (on pp. 145-46) "in both kindes" means both the wine and the bread. No documents have been given from Mary's reign which interrupted the course of the Protestant Reformation.*

*One observes that the expressions of Elizabeth are less belligerent than those of her father. She calls herself not "the supreme head" but the "supreme governor" and she repudiates the authority not of the Bishop of Rome but of any foreign potentate. Latitudinarian as to doctrine, she did demand uniformity in ecclesiastical practices. The*

[7] All of the documents in this reading except in section III are taken from Henry Gee and William John Hardy, *Documents Illustrative of English Church History* (London, 1914), where they are set up in chronological order. All of them are here abridged except the Supremacy Act of 1534. Section III is taken from *The First and Second Prayer-Books of King Edward the Sixth* (Everyman's Library, London, 1910).

*injunctions of the* Advertisements *aroused Puritan ire. The* Act Against Puritans *sought to curb their agitation and the* Act Against Recusants *to keep under surveillance Catholics politically disaffected.*

✓          ✓          ✓

## I. Henry VIII's *First Act of Succession,* 1534

Wherefore we your said most humble and obedient subjects, in this present Parliament assembled, calling to our remembrance the great divisions which in times past have been in this realm, by reason of several titles pretended to the imperial crown of the same, which sometimes, and for the most part ensued, by occasion of ambiguity and doubts, then not so perfectly declared, but that men might, upon froward intents, expound them to every man's sinister appetite and affection, by reason whereof the Bishop of Rome, and see apostolic, contrary to the great and inviolable grants of jurisdictions given by God immediately to emperors, kings and princes, in succession to their heirs, has presumed, in times past, to invest who should please them, to inherit in other men's kingdoms and dominions, which thing we, your most humble subjects, both spiritual and temporal, do most abhor and detest; [*wherefore*] the marriage heretofore solemnized between your highness and the Lady Katherine, being before lawful wife to Prince Arthur, your elder brother, which by him was carnally known, as does duly appear by sufficient proof in a lawful process had and made before Thomas, by the sufferance of God, now archbishop of Canterbury and metropolitan and primate of all this realm, shall be, by authority of this present Parliament, definitely, clearly, and absolutely declared, deemed, and adjudged to be against the laws of Almighty God, and also accepted, reputed, and taken of no value nor effect, but utterly void and annulled.

And for default of such sons of your body begotten, the imperial crown shall be to the issue female, which is the Lady Elizabeth.

## II. *The Supremacy Act,* 1534

Albeit the king's majesty justly and rightfully is and ought to be the supreme head of the Church of England, and so is recognized by the clergy of this realm in their Convocations, yet nevertheless for corroboration and confirmation thereof, and for increase of virtue in Christ's religion within this realm of England, and to repress and extirp all errors, heresies, and other enormities and abuses heretofore used in the same; be it enacted by authority of this present Parliament, that the king our sovereign lord, his heirs and successors, kings of this realm, shall be taken, accepted, and reputed the only supreme head in earth of the Church of England, called *Anglicana Ecclesia;* and shall have and enjoy, annexed and united to the imperial crown of this realm, as well the title and style thereof, as all honours, dignities, pre-eminences, jurisdictions, privileges, authorities, immunities, profits, and commodities to the said dignity of supreme head of the same Church belonging and pertaining; and that our said sovereign lord, his heirs and successors, kings of this realm, shall have full power and authority from time to time to visit, repress, redress, reform, order, correct, restrain, and amend all such errors, heresies, abuses, offences, contempts, and enormities, whatsover they be, which by any manner spiritual authority or jurisdiction ought or may lawfully be reformed, repressed, ordered, redressed, corrected, restrained, or amended, most to the pleasure of Almighty God, the increase of virtue in Christ's religion, and for the conservation of the peace, unity, and tranquillity of this realm; any usage, custom, foreign law, foreign authority, prescription, or any other thing or things to the contrary hereof notwithstanding.

### III. The First and the Second Prayer Books of Edward VI

a. Collects from the first Book of Common Prayer, 1549.

O God, from whom all holy desyres, all good counsayles, and all iuste workes do procede: Geue unto thy seruauntes that peace, which the world cannot geue; that both our hartes maye be sette to obey thy commaundements, and also that by thee we being defended from the feare of oure enemies, may passe oure time in rest and quietnesse; throughe the merites of Jesu Christe our sauiour. Amen

Blessed lord, which hast caused all holy Scriptures to

bee written for our learnyng; graunte us that we maye in suche wise heare them, read, marke, learne, and inwardly digeste them; that by patience, and coumfort of thy holy woorde, we may embrace, and euer hold fast the blessed hope of euerlasting life, which thou hast geuen us in our sauiour Jesus Christe.

Lorde rayse up (we pray the) thy power, and come among us, and with great might succour us; that whereas, through our synnes and wickednes, we be soore lette and hindred, thy bountifull grace and mercye, through the satisfaccion of thy sonne our Lord, may spedily deliuer us; to whom with thee and the holy gost be honor and glory, worlde without ende.

Almyghtye God, whiche haste geuen us thy onlye begotten sonne to take our nature upon hym, and this daye to bee borne of a pure Vyrgyn; Graunte that we beyng regenerate, and made thy children by adoption and grace, maye dailye be renued by thy holy spirite, through the same our Lorde Jesus Christe who lyueth and reygneth &c.

O God, which by the leading of a starre diddest manifest they onelye bebotten sonne to the Gentiles; Mercifully graunt, that we, which know thee now by faith, may after this life haue the fruicion of thy glorious Godhead; through Christe our Lorde.

Lorde we beseche the mercyfullye to receiue the praiers of thy people which cal upon thee; and graunt that they maie both perceaue and knowe what thinges they ought to do, and also haue grace and power faithfully to fulfill the same.

Almyghtye and euerlastyng God, mercifullye looke upon oure infirmities, and in al our daungiers and necessities, stretche foorth thy ryghte hande to helpe and defende us; through Christ our Lorde.

O Lorde whiche doeste teache us that all our doynges withoute charitie are nothyng woorthe; sende by holy ghost, and powre into our heartes that most excellent gyft of charitie, the very bond of peace and al vertues, without the whiche whosoeuer liueth is counted dead before thee: Graunte this for thy onlye sonne, Jesus Christes sake.

Almightie and euerlastynge God, whiche of thy tender loue towarde man, haste sente our sauior Jesus Christ, to take upon him oure fleshe, and to suffre death upon the crosse, that all mankynde shoulde folowe the example of his greate humilitie; mercifully graunte that we both folowe the example of his pacience, and be made partakers of his resurreccion; throughe the same Jesus Christ our lorde.

b. The form for the celebration of the Lord's Supper in the Book of Common Prayer of 1549

*Then shall the Priest turnyng him to gods boord, knele down, and say in the name of all them, that shall receyue the Communion, this prayer folowing.*

We do not presume to come to this thy table (o mercifull lord) trusting in our owne righteousnes, but in thy manifold and great mercies: we be not woorthie so much as to gather up the cromes under thy table: but thou art the same lorde whose propertie is alwayes to haue mercie: Graunt us therefore (gracious lorde) so to eate the fleshe of thy dere sonne Jesus Christ, and to drynke his bloud in these holy Misteries, that we may continuallye dwell in hym, and he in us, that our synfull bodyes may bee made cleane by his body, and our soules washed through hys most precious bloud. Amen.

*Then shall the Prieste firste receiue the Communion in both kindes himselfe, and next deliuer it to other Ministers, if any be there present (that they may bee ready to helpe the chiefe Minister) and after to the people.*

*And when he deliuereth the Sacramente of the body of Christe, he shall say to euery one these woordes.*

The body of our Lorde Jesus Christe whiche was geuen for thee, preserue thy bodye and soule unto euerlasting lyfe.

*And the Minister deliuering the Sacramet of the bloud, and geuing euery one to drinke once and no more, shall say.*

The bloud of our Lorde Jesus Christe which was shed for thee, preserue thy bodye and soule unto euerlastyng lyfe.

c. The same from the Book of Common Prayer of 1552.

*[From the prayer beginning "We do not presume"*
*the words "these holy Misteries" have been omitted.*
*After this prayer the following prayer has been in-*
*serted to stress the points that the Mass is not a*
*sacrifice since Christ was "once offered," and that*
*the rite is a "perpetuall memorye."]*
*Then the Priest standing up shal saye, as foloweth.*

Almighty God oure heauenly father, whiche of thy
tender mercye dyddest geue thine onely sonne Jesus
Christ, to suffre death upon the crosse for our redemp-
cion, who made there (by hys one oblacion of hymselfe
once offered) a full, perfecte and sufficiente sacrifice,
oblacion, and satisfaccion, for the synnes of the whole
worlde, and dyd institute, and in hys holye Gospell com-
maund us to continue, a perpetuall memorye of that his
precious death, untyll hys comynge agayne: Heare us O
mercyefull father wee beeseche thee; and graunt that
wee, receyuing these thy creatures of bread and wyne,
accordinge to thy sonne our Sauioure Jesus Christ's holy
institucion, in remembraunce of his death and passion,
maye be partakers of his most blessed body and bloud:
who, in the same night that he was betrayed, tooke bread,
and when he had geuen thanks, he brake it, and gaue it
to his Disciples, sayinge: Take, eate, this is my bodye
which is geuen for you. Doe this in remembraunce of
me. Lykewyse after supper he tooke the cup, and when
he had geuen thankes, he gaue it to them, sayinge: Drink
ye all of this, for this is my bloud of the new Testament,
whiche is shed for you and for many, for remission of
synnes: do this as oft as ye shal drinke it in remembraunce of me.

*Then shal the minister first receyue the Communion*
*in both kyndes hymselfe, and next deliuer it to other*
*ministers, yf any be there present (that they may*
*help the chief minister) and after to the people in*
*their handes kneling.*

*And when he delyuereth the bread, he shall saye.*

Take and eate this, in remembraunce that Christ dyed
for thee, and feede on him in thy hearte by faythe, with
thankesgeuing.

*And the Minister that delyuereth the cup, shall saye.*

Drinke this in remembraunce that Christ's bloude was shed for thee, and be thankefull.

## IV. Elizabeth's *Supremacy Act,* 1559

a. The oath:

'I, A.B., do utterly testify and declare in my conscience, that the queen's highness is the only supreme governor of this realm, and of all other her highness's dominions and countries, as well in all spiritual or ecclesiastical things or causes, as temporal, and that no foreign prince, person, prelate, state or potentate, has, or ought to have, any jurisdiction, power, superiority, pre-eminence, or authority ecclesiastical or spiritual, within this realm; and therefore I do utterly renounce and forsake all foreign jurisdictions, powers, superiorities, and authorities, and do promise that from henceforth I shall bear faith and true allegiance to the queen's highness, her heirs and lawyful successors, or united and annexed to the imperial crown of this realm. So help me God, and by the contents of this book.'

b. Limitations on authority:

Provided always, and be it enacted by the authority aforesaid, that such person or persons to whom your highness, your heirs or successors, shall hereafter, by letters patent, under the great seal of England, give authority to have or execute any jurisdiction, power, or authority spiritual, or to visit, reform, order, or correct any errors, heresies, schisms, abuses, or enormities by virtue of this Act, shall not in any wise have authority or power to order, determine, or adjudge any matter or cause to be heresy, but only such as heretofore have been determined, ordered, or adjudged to be heresy, by the authority of the canonical Scriptures, or by the first four general Councils, or any of them, or by any other general Council wherein the same was declared heresy by the express and plain words of the said canonical Scriptures, or such as hereafter shall be ordered, judged, or determined to be heresy by the High Court of Parliament of this realm, with the assent of the clergy in their Convocation; anything in this Act contained to the contrary notwithstanding.

## V. *The Advertisements,* 1566

In the ministration of the Holy Communion in cathedral and collegiate churches, the principal minister shall use a cope with gospeller and epistoler agreeably; and at all other prayers to be said at that Communion Table, to use no copes but surplices.

Item, that the dean and prebendaries wear a surplice with a silk hood in the choir; and when they preach in the cathedral or collegiate church, to wear their hood.

Item, that every minister saying any public prayers, or ministering the sacraments or other rites of the Church, shall wear a comely surplice with sleeves, to be provided at the charges of the parish; and that the parish provide a decent table standing on a frame for the Communion Table.

Item, that they shall recently cover with carpet, silk, or other decent covering, and with a fair linen cloth (at the time of the ministration) the Communion Table, and to set the Ten Commandments upon the east wall over the said table.

Item, that all communicants do receive kneeling, and as is appointed by the laws of the realm and the queen's majesty's Injunctions.

Item, that there be none other holy days observed besides the Sundays.

Item, that on Sundays there be no shops open, nor artificers commonly going about their affairs worldly, and that in all fairs and common markets falling upon the Sunday, there be no showing of any wares before the service be done.

### *Articles for outward apparel of persons ecclesiastical*

First, that all archbishops and bishops do use and continue their accustomed apparel.

Item, that all deans of cathedral churches, masters of colleges, all archdeacons, and other dignities in cathedral churches, doctors, bachelors of divinity and law, having any ecclesiastical living, shall wear in their common apparel abroad a side gown with sleeves straight at the hand, without any cuts in the same; and that also without any falling cape; and to wear tippets of sarcenet, as is lawful for them by the Act of Parliament 24 Henry VIII.

Item, that they in their journeying do wear their cloaks with sleeves put on, and like in fashion to their gowns, without guards, welts, or cuts.

Item, that in their private houses and studies they use their own liberty of comely apparel.

Item, that all inferior ecclesiastical persons shall wear long gowns of the fashion aforesaid, and caps as afore is prescribed.

Item, that all poor parsons, vicars, and curates do endeavour themselves to conform their apparel in like sort so soon and as conveniently as their ability will serve to the same. Provided that their ability be judged by the bishop of the diocese. And if their ability will not suffer to buy their long gowns of the form afore prescribed, that then they shall wear their short gowns agreeable to the form before expressed.

## VI. *The Act Against Puritans*, 1593

For the preventing and avoiding of such great inconveniences and perils as might happen and grow by the wicked and dangerous practices of seditious sectaries and disloyal persons; be it enacted by the Queen's most excellent majesty, and by the Lords spiritual and temporal, and the Commons, in this present Parliament assembled, and by the authority of the same, that if any person or persons above the age of sixteen years, which shall obstinately refuse to repair to some church, chapel, or usual place of common prayer, to hear divine service established by her majesty's laws and statutes in that behalf made, and shall forbear to do the same by the space of a month next after, without lawful cause, shall at any time after forty days next after the end of this session of Parliament, by printing, writing, or express words or speeches, advisedly and purposely practise or go about to move or persuade any of her majesty's subjects, or any other within her highness's realms or dominions, to deny, withstand, and impugn her majesty's power and authority in causes ecclesiastical, united, and annexed to the imperial crown of this realm; or to that end or purpose shall advisedly and maliciously move or persuade any other person whatsoever to forbear or abstain from coming to church to hear divine service, or to receive the communion according to her majesty's laws and statutes aforesaid, or to come to or be present at any unlawful assemblies, conventicles, or meetings, under colour or pretence of any exercise of religion, contrary to her majesty's said laws and statutes; then every such person so offending as aforesaid, and being thereof lawfully convicted, shall be committed to prison, there to remain without bail or mainprise, until they shall conform and yield themselves to come to some church.

Provided always, and be it further enacted by the authority aforesaid, that if any such person or persons, which shall offend against this Act as aforesaid, shall not within three months next after they shall be convicted of their said offence, conform themselves to the obedience of the laws and statutes of this realm, in coming to the church to hear divine service, and in making such public confession and submission, that in every such case every such offender shall abjure this realm of England.

## VII. *The Act Against Recusants,* 1593

For the better discovering and avoiding of all such traitorous and most dangerous conspiracies and attempts as are daily devised and practised against our most gracious sovereign lady the queen's majesty and the happy estate of this commonweal, by sundry wicked and seditious persons, who, terming themselves Catholics, and being indeed spies and intelligencers, not only for her majesty's foreign enemies, but also for rebellious and traitorous subjects born within her highness's realms and dominions, and hiding their most detestable and devilish purposes under a false pretext of religion and conscience, do secretly wander and shift from place to place within this realm, to corrupt and seduce her majesty's subjects, and to stir them to sedition and rebellion:

Be it ordained and enacted by our sovereign lady the queen's majesty, and the Lords spiritual and temporal, and the Commons, in this present Parliament assembled, and by the authority of the same, that every person above the age of sixteen years, born within any of the queen's majesty's realms and dominions, or made denizen, being a popish recusant, and before the end of this session of Parliament, convicted for not repairing to some church, chapel, or usual place of common prayer, to hear divine service there, but forbearing the same, contrary to the tenor of the laws and statutes heretofore made and provided in that behalf, and having any certain place of dwelling and abode within this realm, shall within forty days next after the end of this session of Parliament repair to their place of dwelling where they usually heretofore made their common abode, and shall not, any time after, pass or remove above five miles from thence.

— Reading No. 8 —

# THE CATHOLIC REFORMATION[8]

*The three documents following illustrate some of the divergent strains within the Catholic reformatory movement. There were the liberals who desired to reform morals and attenuate or accommodate doctrine and to do all by persuasion, and there were the intransigents, who wished to eradicate laxity in conduct and heresy or even fuzziness of belief, by stringent measures. The first document outlines the moral reforms on which both parties were agreed. Space has precluded an excerpt from the liberal point of view. The writings of Erasmus, easily available in English, afford many examples. The founding of the Jesuits looked in the direction of a victory for the sterner party, because, although the Jesuits were dedicated to education and were lenient toward offenders, yet their utter obedience to their general and to the Pope did not encourage a spirit of free inquiry. The founding of the Inquisition marks the triumph of the tougher policy.*

[8] The documents for this reading were translated from the Latin text in B. J. Kidd, *Documents Illustrative of the Continental Reformation* (Oxford, 1901), (I) No. 126; (II) *Ibid.*, No. 135; (III) *Ibid.*, No. 141.

## I. The Reforms Proposed by the Cardinals
### Addressed to Pope Paul III in 1538

Most blessed Father, we cannot express the gratitude which Christendom should feel toward God for having raised you up in these times as a shepherd to His flock, for the spirit of God has determined through you to restore the falling Church to her pristine sublimity. You have instructed us to declare, without regard for the feelings of yourself or anyone else, those abuses and grievous ailments from which the Church suffers and particularly the Roman Curia. The trouble is that your predecessors surrounded themselves with sychophants, dextrous in proving that whatever they liked was licit. From this Trojan horse issued such ills upon the Church that she is like not to recover. Her ill repute occasions derision among the infidels so that through us the name of Christ is blasphemed among the Gentiles. Since you, most holy Father and truly most holy, are so genuinely concerned to cure these ills, we are laying before you such remedies as our feeble powers can devise. We touch only upon that which affects the Church universal.

To begin with laws should be observed. Nothing is more subversive of laws than dispensations. Nor should the vicar of Christ in exercising the power of the keys have any eye to gain. One abuse is the ordination of priests, even mere lads, utterly unqualified reprobates. No one should be ordained save by a bishop who should have a teacher in his see for clerics in minor orders. Benefices should be conferred only on learned, upright men who will be in residence. An Italian should not be appointed to a post in Spain or Britain. A great abuse is the reservation of revenues designed for the indigent but consigned to the wealthy. The permutation of benefices for gain is simony. By no subterfuge should benefices be treated as legacies. The granting of expectations on benefices engenders the wish that somebody will die. Pluralities, especially in bishoprics, should be abolished and as for the combining of benefices, is not that an evasion of the law? The holding of bishoprics and sometimes several by cardinals is incompatible with their office, because they should assist Your Holiness in the

governance of the Church universal, whereas a bishop
should look after his flock. How is the Holy See to correct the abuses of others if there be so many in the
chief members? Nothing is more important, blessed
Father, than that bishops should reside in their sees.
What more grievous sight could afflict a traveler throughout Christendom than to view so many neglected
churches? Equally is it an abuse that the cardinals should
reside in their provinces rather than here at Rome. By
the blood of Christ we beseech Your Holiness not to
suborn the authority of the bishops by suffering priests
under discipline to escape through appeal. Confessors
should be appointed not by friars but by bishops. A most
pernicious abuse is the teaching of impiety by professors
in the universities and especially in Italy. The *Colloquies*
of Erasmus should not be used for the instruction of
youth. Apostate monks, who have abandoned their hab-
its, should not be given dispensations for money. Dispensations should not be given to those in holy orders to
marry unless it be to retain an entire people in the faith,
especially in these days when the Lutherans so insistently
demand clerical marriage. Dispensations for marriage
should not be given in the second degree and in the
other degrees only for good cause and without money.
Absolution should not be given for simony. There are
those who having committed it, then buy absolution and
retain the benefice purchased. Portable confessionals are
not approved. Indulgences should not be allowed in a
given territory more than once a year. Commutation of
vows is not approved. Testaments are not to be altered
unless some grave change has occurred in the fortunes of
the family. Since Rome is the mother of the churches it
is scandalous that the priests officiating in St. Peter's are
ignorant and filthy. In this city prostitutes are conveyed
like matrons by mules followed by cardinals and clerics.
This shameful abuse must be ended. The cardinals should
endeavor to compose feuds between Roman citizens.
There are in this city hospitals and widows who should
be your especial care.

Blessed Father, these are our modest proposals to be
tempered by your goodness and wisdom. You have taken
the name of Paul. May you imitate the love of Paul that
you may make the Church a washed and spotless dove.

## II. The Founding of the Jesuits, 1539

*Ten young men including Ignatius Loyola and Francis Xavier, the best known in the group, applied to the Pope for recognition as a religious order. The Pope reviewed their worthy record and then gave his approval to the oath which Loyola had proposed, namely:*

Whoever wishes to be a warrior of God under the banner of the cross in our society, which bears the name of Jesus, to serve God alone and His vicar on earth, the Roman Pontiff, must after taking the solemn vow of perpetual chastity dedicate himself to propagate the faith through public preaching and ministry of the Word of God, spiritual exercises and works of piety and particularly the religious education of children, by affording spiritual consolation through the hearing of confessions. He must keep constantly God before his eyes, striving to attain the goal set him by God and to fulfill those rules which are in a sense a way to God. Lest any behave with excessive zeal let each member place himself entirely under the direction of the general or prelates chosen by us. This general shall have authority to establish a constitution in conclave where the decision of the majority shall prevail. In major matters a majority of the entire membership must be present; in minor affairs those who happen to be at hand. Let every member recognize that not only when he makes his profession, but throughout his life, he is subject to the present Pope and to his successors. We are bound beyond the ordinary by a particular vow in this regard. If then the present Pope or his successors should send us for the improvement of souls or the propagation of the faith to the Turks or other infidels even in India or to heretics, schismatics or some of the faithful, we are to obey without evasion or excuse. Wherefore, those who would join us should consider long before taking this load upon their shoulders and should well count the cost whether they have sufficient spiritual wealth to build the tower. In everything touching the rule, let obedience be given to the general. He in turn is always to be mindful of the goodness, gentleness, and love of Christ. All should be concerned for the instruction of youth in Christian doctrine and the Ten Commandments. Since we have discovered a life of poverty to be more conducive to happiness, purity and edification, we vow ourselves to perpetual poverty not only singly but as an order in the sense that there is to be no legal holding but rather contentment with gifts covering necessities, except that in schools it is permissible to have whatever is necessary for students.

### III. The Establishment of the Roman Inquisition by Paul III, July 21, 1542

Although from the beginning of our Pontificate we have been concerned for the flourishing of the Catholic faith and the expurgation of heresy that those seduced by diabolical wiles might return to the fold and unity of the Church and that those who persist in their damnable course should be removed and their punishment might serve as an example to others, nevertheless hoping that the mercy of God, the prayers of the faithful and the preaching of the learned would cause them to recognize their errors and come back to the Holy Catholic Church, and if any delayed they would be induced by the authority of the sacred, ecumenical and general council, which we hope speedily to convene, therefore we deferred the establishment of the Inquisition of heretical Pravity, but now, since for a variety of reasons, the council has not met and the enemy of the human race has disseminated even more heresy among the faithful and the robe of Christ is further rent, consequently, lest pending a council things grow worse, we have appointed our beloved sons, Giovanni Caraffa [and five others], Inquisitors General with jurisdiction throughout Christendom including Italy and the Roman Curia. They are to investigate by way of inquisition all and single who wander from the way of the Lord and the Catholic faith, as well as those suspected of heresy, together with their followers and abettors, public or private, direct or indirect. The guilty and the suspects are to be imprisoned and proceeded against up to the final sentence. Those adjudged guilty are to be punished in accord with canonical penalties. After the infliction of death goods may be put up for sale. The aid of the civil arm may be invoked to implement whatever measures the above named deem needful. Any who impede will incur the indignation of Almighty God and of the blessed Apostles, Peter and Paul.

## — Reading No. 9 —

## CONFESSIONS OF FAITH[9]

*The three confessions, abridged here are Lutheran, Anglican, and Catholic. The full text will be found in Philip Schaff, Creeds of Christendom. Likewise one will find there Calvinist confessions emanating from France, Scotland, and Holland. All of these confessions aim to give the main points of affirmative belief. Yet, since they were elicited by opposition, they devote also much space to refutation. They are in a measure conditioned by each other and they have an eye to political exigencies.*

*The Augsburg Confession went, as far as loyalty to conviction would permit, in the direction of agreement with the Church of Rome. The affirmative portion of the Confession is digested here. The negative portion certainly repudiates Roman teaching unequivocally at many points. The Thirty-Nine Articles came after the Augsburg Confession, and what is more, after it had received recognition by the Empire in certain sections of Germany. To stay within its compass was for Elizabeth a point of political strategy. Still one does sense something of a Calvinist tone in what is said on predestination. The Council of Trent was much concerned to repudiate Protestant errors and in the excerpts given roundly rejects Lutheran views as to the sacraments and the priesthood. The formulation of the doctrine of justification by faith is not included here. For this consult the text in the work of Schaff above mentioned.*

[9] The documents for this reading are: (I) Translated from the Latin text by Philip Schaff, *Creeds of Christendom* 3 (New York, 1877), pp. 3-73, greatly condensed; (II) *Ibid.*, p. 486 f.; (III) *Translations and Reprints from Original Sources of European History: Period of the Early Reformation in Germany,* ed. James Harvey Robinson and Merrick Whitcomb, published by the Department of History of the University of Pennsylvania, Philadelphia, 2, 6 (January, 1908), pp. 34-36.

## I. *The Augsburg Confession*, 1530

*The Augsburg Confession divides into two parts. As mentioned above, the first has the principal articles of faith and the second a refutation of the abuses in the Catholic Church. Nevertheless, in the first part there are many repudiations of Anabaptist teachings. These portions are omitted here. The following gathers up the main points of the first half.*

1) Of God: The churches with common consent among us do teach that the decree of the Nicene Synod concerning the unity of the divine essence and of the three persons is true. 2) Of original sin: Also they teach that after Adam's fall all men begotten after the common course of nature are born with sin, that is without the fear of God, without trust in Him and with fleshly appetite; and that this disease or original fault is truly sin condemning and bringing eternal death now also upon all that are not born again by baptism and the Holy Spirit. 3) Of the Son of God. [*This section is a paraphrase of the Apostles' Creed.*] 4) Justification: Men cannot be justified before God by their own power, merits or works; but are justified freely for Christ's sake through faith. 5) Of the ministry: For the obtaining of this faith the ministry of teaching the Gospel and administering the sacraments was instituted. 6) This faith should bring forth good fruits. Men ought to do the good works commanded by God because it is God's will and not on any confidence of meriting justification before God by their works. 7) The Church is the congregation of saints in which the Gospel is purely preached and the sacraments rightly administered. 8) Baptism is necessary to salvation. Children are to be baptized. 10) In the Lord's Supper the true body and blood of Christ are present under the form of bread and wine. 11) Concerning confession: Private absolution may be retained in the churches, though enumeration of all offenses is not necessary in confession. 16) Concerning civil affairs: Christians may lawfully bear civil office, sit in judgment, determine matters by imperial law, appoint just punishments, engage in just war, act as soldiers, make legal con-

tracts, hold property, take an oath when the magistrates require it, marry a wife or be given in marriage. 18) Concerning free will: Man's will hath some liberty to work a civil righteousness and to choose such things as reason can reach unto; but it hath no power to work the righteousness of God without the spirit of God.

## II. The *Thirty-Nine Articles* of the Church of England, 1562

*The first articles are entitled: Of fayth in the holy Trinitie, Of the worde or sonne of God which was made very man, Of the goyng downe of Christe into hell, Of the Resurrection of Christe, Of the holy ghost, Of the sufficiencie of the Holy Scriptures for saluation. Then follows a list of the canonical books of the Old Testament including the Apocrypha which, however, is not to be used to establish doctrine.*

✓          ✓          ✓

ARTICLE 7) The olde Testament is not contrary to the newe. 8) Three Credes are professed: the Apostles', the Nicene and the Athanasian. 9) Originall sinne standeth not in the following of Adam. It is the fault and corruption of the nature of euery man, that naturally is engendered of the ofspring of Adam. 10) The condition of man after the fall of Adam is suche, that he can not turne and prepare hym selfe by his owne naturall strength and good workes, to fayth and calling vpon God. 11) We are accompted righteous before God, only for the merite of our Lord and sauiour Jesus Christe, by faith. 12) Albeit that good workes which are the fruites of fayth, . . . can not put away our sinnes yet are they pleasing and acceptable to God in Christe. 13) Workes done before the grace of Christe we doubt not but they haue the nature of synne. 14) Voluntarie workes besydes, ouer and aboue Gods commaundementes, which they call workes of supererogation, can not be taught without arrogancie and impietie. 17) Predestination to lyfe, is the euerlastyng purpose of God, whereby (before the foundations of the world were layd) he hath constantly decreed by his councell secrete to vs, to deliuer from curse and damnation, those whom he hath chosen in Christe out of mankynd. As the godly consyderation of predestination, and our election in Christe, is full of sweete, pleasaunt, and vnspeakeable comfort to godly persons, so, for curious and carnal persons to haue continually before their eyes the sentence of Gods predestination, is a most daungerous downefall. 19) The visible Church of Christe, is a congregation of faythfull men in the which the pure worde of God is preached, and the Sacramentes be duely ministred. 20) The Church hath power to decree Rites or Ceremonies, and aucthoritie in controuersies of fayth. [*This last phrase was added by the Queen*]. 21) Generall Counsels may not be gathered without the commaundement and wyll of princes. And when they be gathered they may erre. 25) Sacramentes ordayned of Christe be certaine sure witnesses and effectuall signes of grace and Gods good wyll towardes vs. There are two Sacramentes ordayned of Christe. Baptisme, and the Supper of the Lorde. 27) Baptisme is a signe of regeneration or newe byrth. The baptisme of young children, is in any wyse to be retayned in the Churche. 28) The Supper of the Lord is a parttakyng of the body of Christe, and likewyse the cuppe of blessing, is a parttakyng of the blood of Christe. Transubstantiation is repugnaunt to the playne wordes of scripture. The body of Christe is geuen, taken, and eaten in the Supper only after an heauenly and spirituall maner. 29) The wicked in no wyse are the partakers of Christe [*This article was suppressed by the Queen until 1571*]. 32) Byshops, Priestes, and Deacons, are not commaunded by Gods lawe eyther to vowe the estate of single lyfe, or to abstayne from mariage. 37) The Queenes Maiestie hath the cheefe power in this Realme of Englande. We geue not to our princes the ministring either of God's word, or of Sacraments. It is lawfull for Christian men, at the commaundement of the Magistrate, to weare weapons, and serue in the warres. 39) A man may sweare when the Magistrate requireth, in a cause of faith and charitie.

### III. Examples of the Canons of the Council of Trent, 1545

*Twenty-third Session, Chapter IV.*—Inasmuch as in the sacrament of Orders, as also in Baptism and Confirmation, a character is imprinted which can neither be effaced nor taken away, this holy council with reason condemns the opinions of those who assert that the priests of the New Testament have only a temporary power; and that those who have once been properly ordained can again become laymen, if they do not exercise the ministry of God. And if anyone affirm that all Christians indiscriminately are priests of the New Testament, or that they are all mutually endowed with an equal spiritual power, he clearly does nothing but confound the ecclesiastical hierarchy,—which is "as an army set in array;"—as if, contrary to the doctrine of blessed Paul, "all were apostles, all prophets, all evangelists, all pastors, all doctors." Wherefore this holy Synod declares that, besides the other ecclesiastical degrees, bishops, who have succeeded to the place of the apostles, especially belong to this hierarchical order; that they are placed, as the same apostle says, "by the Holy Ghost, to rule the Church of God," that they are superior to priests, administer the sacrament of Confirmation, ordain the ministers of the Church; and that they can perform very many other things, over which functions others of an inferior order have no power. Furthermore, the sacred and holy synod teaches that, in the ordination of bishops, priests, and of the other orders, neither the consent, nor vocation, nor authority, whether of the people or of any civil power or magistrate whatsoever, is required in such wise that, without this, the ordination is invalid: nay, rather doth it decree that all those who being once called and instituted by the people, or by the civil power and magistrate, ascend to the exercise of the ministrations, and those who of their own rashness assume them to themselves, are not ministers of the Church, but are to be looked upon as "thieves and robbers, who have not entered by the door."

*Twenty-third Session, Canon I.*—If any one shall say that the New Testament does not provide for a distinct, visible priesthood, or that this priesthood has no power to consecrate and offer up the true body and blood of the Lord, or remit or refuse to remit sins, but that its sole function is that of preaching the Gospel, and that those who do not preach are not priests, let him be anathema.

*Twenty-third Session, Canon IV.*—If any shall say that the Holy Spirit is not given by holy ordination and that consequently the Bishops say in vain "Receive ye the Holy Spirit," and that certain characteristics are not thereby conferred, or that he who has once been a priest can ever be made a layman again, let him be anathema.

*Seventh Session, Of the Sacraments, Canon I.*—If any one saith that the sacraments of the New Law were not all instituted by Jesus Christ, our Lord; or that they are more or less than seven, to-wit, Baptism, Confirmation, the Eucharist, Penance, Extreme Unction, Orders and Matrimony; or even that any one of these seven is not truly and properly a sacrament, let him be anathema.

*Canon VI.*—If anyone saith that the sacraments of the New Law do not contain the grace which they signify; or that they do not confer that grace on those who do not place an obstacle thereunto; as though they were merely outward signs of grace or justice received through faith, and certain marks of the Christian profession, whereby believers are distinguished amongst men from unbelievers, let him be anathema.

*Canon VIII.*—If anyone saith that by the said sacraments of the New Law grace is not conferred through the very performance of the act [*ex opere operato*], but that faith alone in the divine promise suffices for the obtaining of grace, let him be anathema.

*Canon IX.*—If anyone saith that in the three sacraments, to-wit, Baptism, Confirmation, and Orders, there is not imprinted in the soul a character, that is, a spiritual and indelible sign, on account of which they cannot be repeated, let him be anathema.

*Canon X.*—If anyone saith that all Christians have power to administer the word and all the sacraments, let him be anathema.

*Canon XII.*—If anyone saith that a minister, being in mortal sin—if so be that he observe all the essentials which belong to the effecting or conferring of the sacrament—neither effects nor confers the sacraments, let him be anathema.

*Thirteenth Session, Chapter IV.*—Since Christ our Redeemer declared that it was truly his body which he offered up in the form [*sub specie*] of bread, and since the Church has moreover always accepted this belief, this holy council declares once more that by the consecration of the bread and the wine the whole substance of the bread is converted into the substance of the body of Christ our Lord, and the whole substance of the wine into the substance of his blood, which change is aptly and properly termed transubstantiation by the Catholic Church.

*Thirteenth Session, Canon I.*—If any one shall deny that the body and blood of our Lord Jesus Christ together with his spirit and divinity, to-wit, Christ all in all, are not truly, really and materially contained in the holy sacrament of the Eucharist, and shall assert that the Eucharist is but a symbol or figure, let him be anathema.

*Thirteenth Session, Canon VI.*—If any one shall say that Christ, the only-begotten son of God, is not to be worshipped with the highest form of adoration [*Latria*] including external worship, in the holy sacrament of the Eucharist, or that the Eucharist should not be celebrated by a special festival, nor borne solemnly about in procession according to the praiseworthy and universal rite and custom of the holy Church, nor held up publicly for the veneration of the people and that those who adore it are idolaters, let him be anathema.

*Twenty-Second Session, Canon III.*—If any one shall say that the sacrifice of the Mass is only a praiseworthy deed or act of edification, or that it is simply in commemoration of the sacrifice on the cross and is not in the nature of a propitiation; or that it can benefit only him who receives it, and ought not to be offered for the living and the dead, for sins, punishment, atonement and other necessary things, let him be anathema.

# EDICTS AFFECTING RELIGION[10]

*The edicts affecting religion in the sixteenth century here excerpted begin with severity and end with moderation. The first placed Luther under the ban of the empire. Inability to enforce the decree led to some relaxation in the years immediately following. The Diet of Speier in 1529 resolved to arrest the consequent spread of Lutheranism and enjoined the enforcement of the Edict of Worms in so far as this might be politically feasible. This elicited the famous protest, from which originated the name "Protestant." The Recess of the Diet of Augsburg in 1530 was only a truce. A solution of the religious problem along territorial lines was first achieved in Switzerland at Cappell in 1531. The same solution was not adopted in Germany until the Peace of Augsburg in 1555 when the Lutheranism attained recognition in designated areas. The Consensus of Sandomir introduced a new principle in that three confessions accorded each*

[10] The documents in this reading were taken from: (I) Translation by R. H. Bainton in *Here I Stand* (New York, 1950), p. 189 from *Deutsche Reichstagsakten* II, No. 92; (II) Kidd, *op. cit.*, No. 69; (III) From the German in the St. Louis edition of Luther's Works [a reprint of Walch] XVI, No. 809, s. 4, col. 210; (IV) The Protest of April 19 is translated in B. J. Kidd, *op. cit.*, No. 107, The Protest of April 20 is translated in full by Henry C. Vedder, Crozer Historical Leaflets No. 1. This protest, actually the third is here greatly condensed and translated from the German in the *Deutsche Reichstagsakten* VII, No. 137; Translated in B. J. Kidd, *op. cit.*, No. 105; (V) Translated from the Latin Text in *Ibid.*, No. 123; (VI) *Ibid.*, No. 227; (VII) Translated from the Latin in *Ibid.*, No. 125; (VIII) Translated from the German text published by Karl Brandi, *Der Augsburger Religionsfriede* (Munich, 1896); (IX) From the Latin in Kidd, *op. cit.*, No. 322; (X) Condensed from the translation in James Fontaine, *Memoirs of a Huguenot Family* (New York, 1853), appendix.

*other mutual recognition without territorial division. The
Edict of Nantes was something of a combination of
mutual recognition and territorialism. The Huguenots
enjoyed full liberty of religion only in specified places.
Nevertheless, as to public office, they were on a par with
Catholics throughout the realm. The degree of liberty
thus far achieved applied to confessions rather than to
individuals. On the two last-mentioned settlements consult Archibald Smith Foord and Thomas Mendenhall
"Historical Revisions—The Peace of Augsburg—The
Edict of Nantes,"* The New England Social Studies Bul-
letin, *IX (1952), pp. i-ii.*

✓ ✓ ✓

## I. The Edict of Worms Presented to the Diet
by the Emperor, May 6, 1521

Luther has sullied marriage, disparaged confession,
and denied the body and blood of our Lord. He makes
the sacraments depend on the faith of the recipient. He
is pagan in his denial of free will. This devil in the habit
of a monk has brought together ancient errors into one
stinking puddle and has invented new ones. He denies
the power of the keys and encourages the laity to wash
their hands in the blood of the clergy. His teaching
makes for rebellion, division, war, murder, robbery,
arson, and the collapse of Christendom. He lives the
life of a beast. He has burned the decretals. He despises
alike the ban and the sword. He does more harm to the
civil than to the ecclesiastical power. We have labored
with him, but he recognizes only the authority of Scripture, which he interprets in his own sense. We have given
him twenty-one days, dating from April the 25th. We
have now gathered the estates. Luther is to be regarded
as a convicted heretic [*although the bull of excommunication still had not been published*]. When the time is up,
no one is to harbor him. His followers also are to be
condemned. His books are to be eradicated from the
memory of man.

## II. The Recess of the Diet of Nürnberg,
April 18, 1524

Neglect to enforce our edict promulgated at Worms
had occasioned no little detriment to Christendom and to

the entire German nation. Therefore, we called again upon each of the electors, etc. that for himself and his subjects he should see to it that the Edict of Worms be obediently observed. The electors then acknowledged themselves so bound, and they agreed among themselves with all their might to enforce the edict insofar as might be possible and no scurrilous books or cartoons were to be issued.

### III. The Recess of the Diet of Speier, August 27, 1526

Thereafter, we, the electors, princes, and estates, and their representatives here assembled at this Diet, have unanimously agreed that pending a council or a national assembly, we together with our subjects in matters affecting the edict promulgated by his imperial majesty at Worms will so live, rule, and behave as each hopes and trusts to answer before God and his imperial majesty.

### IV. The Protest at the Diet of Speier, April 20, 1529

*The following protest was directed against a resolution of the majority of the Diet on April 7, 1529 which declared that the Edict of Worms was to be enforced. Tacit toleration was given to those Lutheran areas in which enforcement would entail considerable "tumult, trouble and danger." But in these areas no further innovation was to be allowed, whereas in the Lutheran territories the celebration of the Mass must be permitted. In other words, no Lutheran practices would be tolerated in Catholic territory, but Catholic practices must be suffered in the Lutheran. Against this resolution the minority protested as follows:*

✦              ✦              ✦

Inasmuch as your royal highness and your representatives as well as the electors, princes, and estates of the empire agreed unanimously at Speier as touching the Edict of Worms that for the peace of the realm until the meeting of a general council or a national assembly each elector, prince, and estate with their subjects should "so live, rule, and behave as each hopes and trusts to answer to God and his imperial majesty," we cannot and we will not consent to the abrogation of the above mentioned unanimous agreement. If this third declaration of our grave objections receives no consideration from your Majesty and the rest, then we protest and testify herewith publicly before God, our sole creator, preserver, redeemer, and saviour, who alone searches the secrets of all hearts and renders just judgment to all men and creatures that for ourselves and our subjects one and all we deem the said recess to be null and void as contrary to God, His Word, our soul's salvation, our consciences and also contrary to the former recess of the Diet of Speier, but we will, as there decreed, conduct ourselves until the meeting of the general council or a national assembly as we hope to answer to God and to you.

### V. The Recess of the Diet of Augsburg, September 22, 1530

After his imperial majesty had convened a Diet of the Estates in Augsburg on the eighth day of April last to take cognizance of the affairs of the empire, the Christian world and the German nation and particularly to deliberate concerning the holy faith in the Christian religion that as we fight under one Christ, so we may all dwell in unity and concord in one Church, at this Diet the emperor, the electors, and the princes permitted the Elector of Saxony, George the Duke of Saxony, the brothers Ernest and Francis Dukes of Lüneberg, Philip the Langrave of Hesse, Wolfgang Prince of Anhalt, and the cities of Nürnberg, Reutlingen, Kempten, Heilbronn, Windsheim, and Weissenburg to submit a confession. This statement has been subjected to careful scrutiny and refuted by the firm testimonies of Holy Scripture. The emperor then, out of love for public peace and tranquility, especially in Germany and out of singular benignity, and clemency grants to the Elector of Saxony, the five princes, and the six cities a period of deliberation until the 15th of April next that they may decide whether or no they will accord with the pope, the emperor, the other electors and the princes and the entire Christian world until the meeting of a council. In the meantime peace shall be kept throughout the empire. The Saxon and his associates are to print and publish nothing about religion throughout their domains. They shall compel none to their religion nor impede the practice of the old and shall not interfere with monks and nuns in the hearing of confession and the hearing of Mass.

### VI. The Second Peace of Cappel, November 20, 1531

First, we of Zürich shall and will let our trusty and well beloved Confederates of the Five Cantons abide without any contradiction or dispute in their true, undoubted Christian faith [*Catholicism*], and we in our turn of the Five Cantons will let our Confederates of Zürich abide by their faith.

### VII. The Peace of Nürnberg, July 23, 1532

Albert, by the grace of God Elector of the Holy Roman Empire, Cardinal, Legate, Archbishop of Mainz, and Magdeburg, Archchancellor and Primate of Germany [etc.] and Ludwig, Elector Palatine [etc.] testify that when discord over religion broke out between our invincible Emperor Charles on the one side and the illustrious princes on the other, namely our beloved cousins, the Elector of Saxony [a full list] we endeavored to compose these differences but without avail. And since the Turk could not be resisted if there were not unity in the Empire, with all due reverence, we besought his Imperial Majesty to summon a general, free, Christian council and, if that were impossible, then a Diet of the Empire. And in the meantime none should make war on account of religion. The Emperor then out of regard for the public peace graciously promised to strive for the summoning of a council within six months to commence its sessions within a year. And he promised that any measures commenced or contemplated against the Elector of Saxony and his allies would be suspended until the meeting of a future council and on their part likewise our cousins, the Elector of Saxony, the Duke of Lüneberg and their allies promise to observe the public peace and to show the Emperor due reverence, obedience, and to aid in resisting the Turks.

### VIII. The Peace of Augsburg, September 25, 1555

1) Inasmuch as for the last thirty years continuous but

unsuccessful efforts have been made to allay the dissensions arising by reason of religion, in order that our beloved German fatherland may not be rent and ruined we have agreed with the electors, princes, estates, and ambassadors that no one whosoever for any reason whatsoever shall attack, rob, molest or beleaguer any castle, town, market, stronghold, or village or impede free interchange but shall preserve the peace in accord with the following religious constitution. 3) To this end the emperor, electors, princes, and estates of the Holy Roman Empire shall not molest any adherents of the Augsburg Confession on account of their religion nor by force seek to persuade, damage, or compel them against their conscience, knowledge, and will to renounce this Augsburg Confession, but religious differences shall be settled in a Christian, friendly, and peaceful manner under penalty of the imperial ban. 4) Similarly those who adhere to this Confession shall not molest the emperor, electors, princes, and other estates who abide by the old religion and shall not interfere with their faith, practices, ordinances, and ceremonies nor with their properties and governments under penalty of the imperial ban. 5) But those who do not hold to either of the above mentioned religions shall be totally excluded from this peace. 6) If in future any archbishop, bishop, prelate or other ecclesiastic should decide to leave the old religion, he must renounce all of his benefices in favor of one who does profess the old religion. 7) Any foundation, cloisters, or any other ecclesiastical goods which were not in the possession of the clergy at the time of the Treaty of Passau are not to be restored. 10) No estate shall try to force another or its subjects to its own religion and shall not abet any of such subjects against their own government. 11) But if any of the subjects in the territories confessing the old religion or the Augsburg Confession wish to emigrate with wife and child they shall be free to go unmolested and to sell their goods at current rates. 14) But inasmuch as in some of the free cities both religions already exist side by side, this arrangement shall continue and neither shall disturb the other. 15) Anything contrary to these enactments up to the Treat of Passau is annulled.

## IX. The Consensus of Sandomir,
### April 14, 1570

After that we have been greatly troubled by sectaries, Tritheists, Ebionites and Anabaptists, and yet by divine favor have emerged from such deplorable contentions, it has seemed good to the reformed and orthodox churches of Poland [*Calvinist*] in the interests of peace and concord to convoke a synod. We are agreed on the following points. First, we who in the present synod have made our confession [*the Calvinists and the Brethren that is, the Bohemian Hussites*] never have held that those who adhered to the Augsburg Confession entertained other than godly and orthodox views of God, the Holy Trinity, and the incarnation of the Son of God, our justification, and other principle points of the faith and likewise they of the Augsburg Confession sincerely confess that our churches and the Bohemian Brethren (erroneously called Waldenses) hold nothing incompatible with orthodox truth on the above points.

## X. The Edict of Nantes, April, 1598

Catholics have complained that in some of their towns their religion has not been reëstablished and the Reformed have complained that promises to them remain unfulfilled. The memory of the past on both sides beginning with March 1585 is to be forgotten. Our subjects must not offend one another. We command that in all places of our kingdom where the exercise of the apostolic Roman Catholic religion has been interrupted it shall be reëstablished. All who during the troubles became possessed of properties of clergymen shall restore them. 6) We permit those of the Pretended Reformed Religion to live and remain in all cities and places without being disturbed, vexed, molested, or forced to do anything against their conscience on the subject of religion. Neither can their houses or places of abode be searched on that score. 7) We have permitted all lords and nobles professing the Pretended Reformed Religion having jurisdiction in manorial courts to exercise the said religion in such houses as they shall designate as the principal domicile. 8) Where those of the said religion do not have such jurisdiction they may have worship in their own families and witn guests not to exceed thirty provided the localities are not in the cities, towns, or villages belonging to Catholic noblemen. 10) We also permit those of the said religion to continue its exercise in all places where it was established before the end of August, 1597. It may also be restored in all places where it was or had the right to be established by the pacification of 1577. 13) We expressly forbid any religious exercises [of the Reformed] except in places designated in this edict. 15) The public exercise of the said religion cannot be permitted in the army except at the quarters of those generals who profess it. 17) We forbid all preachers inciting to sedition. 18) We forbid taking children by force to have them baptized in the apostolic Roman Catholic Church or vice versa. 21) Books of the Pretended Reformed Religion may be printed in towns where the exercise of this religion is allowed. Scandalous books are forbidden. 27) Those of the Pretended Reformed Religion shall be eligible for all public offices and membership in all councils and assemblies. 28) Provision is to be made for the burial of the dead of the Reformed and cemeteries formerly in their possession are to be restored. 70) The children of those who quit the kingdom for religion, even though born out of the kingdom of France, shall enjoy all the rights and privileges of native Frenchmen. 73) If any prisoners are still confined in the galleys on account of the troubles they are to be released. 82) All associations in the provinces contrary to the present edict must be annulled.

*Secret articles.* 1) The article on religious liberty is to include all ministers and schoolmasters. 39) Marriages of priests and nuns shall not be disturbed. 53) His majesty will instruct his ambassadors to solicit for all his subjects traveling in foreign countries from forcing of conscience and the Inquisition.

*The Writ of April 31st.* To those of the Pretended Reformed Religion his Majesty has granted all places, cities, and castles of which they had possession until the end of August last in which they shall have garrisons and a list shall be drawn up and signed by his Majesty and shall remain in their keeping under the authority of his Majesty for the space of eight years to count from the day of the publication of this edict. For the support of said garrisons his Majesty has granted one hundred and eighty thousand pounds.

# — Reading No. 11 —

## THE RIGHT OF REBELLION[11]

*The attempts by force in the sixteenth century to sup-
press religion occasioned an examination afresh of the
authority of rulers. The Protestants were all clear that
any command contrary to God's Word must be dis-
obeyed. But to go further and by arms to resist the ruler
was a more drastic step which gave rise to grave searching of heart. The statement of the Apostle Paul that
rulers are ordained of God* (Romans 13) *would seem to
preclude any right of revolution. The device for escaping
this conclusion was to pit a ruler against a ruler, a lower
magistrate against a higher. This was the solution of the*
Magdeburg Bekenntnis. *In Germany this meant the
electors, or the princes against the emperor. In France
the princes of the blood might resist the crown. Calvin,
as we have seen* (see Reading 6, No. VI (C)), *discountenanced the Conspiracy of Amboise, because it was
not led by a prince of the blood. In England in the
Cromwellian period the position of the lower magistrate
was assigned to Parliament, but under Mary Tudor Parliament could not be counted on to essay any such role
in England, nor would the corresponding body in Scotland. Consequently, Ponet, Goodman and Knox advance
a more radical theory. Ponet is very loath to have the
private individual wield the sword against the ruler. He*

[11] The documents in this reading are taken from: (I) *Bekenntnis Unterricht und Vermanung/der Pfarrhern und Pre-
diger/der Christlichen Kirchen zu Magdeburgk,* Anno
1550 den 13 Aprilis (Magdeburg, **1550**). Greatly condensed; (II) Facsimile edition by **Winthrop** S. Hudson,
1942, pp. 111-12; (III) Facsimile Text Society (New
York, 1931), pp. 179-81; (IV) John Knox, *The History
of the Reformation within the Realm of Scotland 1559-
1571,* Reprint ed. C. J. Guthrie Ld., 1898, pp. 271-82;
(V) *Vindiciae contra tyrannos* (1581), English translation 1689, reprint London 1924 with an introduction by
Harold Laski. Sentences culled with the order retained.

*may do so if specially inspired—this was the current device employed to explain the deviations of the Patriarchs in the Old Testament from the standards of Christian morality. But even without such a call, the citizen may step in if the ruler contemplates the utter subversion of the country and all others in the state are completely supine. Goodman is more radical. The power of magistracy is distributed throughout the community and, if magistrates betray justice, common citizens become magistrates. Knox is less theoretical. For him power is a derivative of truth. If magistrates suppress truth subjects are commissioned by God to resist.* The Defence of Liberty Against Tyrants *brings in contractual ideas.*

✔          ✔          ✔

## I. *The Confession of Magdeburg* (Lutheran), 1550

We will undertake to show that a Christian government may and should defend its subjects against a higher authority which should try to compel the people to deny God's Word and to practice idolatry. We scarcely expect to convince the Catholics that subjects may resist their Lord and a lower magistrate may resist a higher if he seeks to uproot the Christian religion, for the Catholics do not admit that we have the Christian religion and consequently think they have the right to make war upon us. Our object is primarily to allay the scruples of those who do adhere to the true Word of God. But first we would address ourselves to the Emperor and beg him not to let the Pope persecute the Lord, Christ. But if your Majesty will not concede that Lutherans are Christians, bear in mind that Christ was considered a blasphemer, and He has shown us one mark of the true Church, namely, that it should not constrain anyone with the sword as the Roman Church does. Obedience to God and to Caesar are not incompatible, provided each stays within his own proper sphere. Your Majesty has gone beyond your office and encroached upon the kingdom of Christ. Your present dissatisfaction with us is no one's fault but your own, and we may say to you in the words of Elijah to Ahab, "It is not I that troubles Israel but you."

We will show from Holy Scripture that if a higher magistrate undertakes by force to restore popish idolatry and to suppress or exterminate the pure teaching of the Holy Gospel, as in the present instance, then the lower godfearing magistrate may defend himself and his subjects against such unjust force in order to preserve the true teaching, the worship of God together with body, life, goods, and honor. The powers that be are ordained of God to protect the good and punish the bad (*Romans 13*), but if they start to persecute the good, they are no longer ordained of God. There are to be sure degrees of tyranny and if a magistrate makes unjust war upon his subjects contrary to his plighted oath, they may resist, though they are not commanded to do so by God. But if a ruler is so demented as to attack God, then he is the very devil who employs mighty potentates in Church and State. When, for example, a prince or an emperor tampers with marriage against the dictates of natural law, then in the name of natural law and Scripture he may be resisted.

Praise be to God. Because He lives we also shall live and be exalted since now we suffer with Him and for his sake we are killed all the day long (*Psalm 44*).

## II. John Ponet: *A Shorte Treatise of Politike Power,* 1556

And Christ pronounceth, that euery tree which bringeth not furthe good frute, shalbe cut downe, and cast in to the fire: muche more the euil tree, that bringeth furthe euil frute. And albeit some doo holde, that the maner and meane to punishe euil and euil doers, is not all one among Christianes (which be in dede that they professe in worde) and Ethnikes, which thinke it lauful for euery priuate man (without respecte of ordre and time) to punishe euil: yet the lawes of many christiane regiones doo permitte, that priuate men maie kil malefactours, yea though they were magistrates, in some cases: as whan a gouernour shall sodainly with his sworde renne upon an innocent, or goo about to shoote him through with a gonne, or if he should be founde in bedde with a mannes wife, or goo about to defloure and rauishe a mannes daughther: muche more if [*he*] goo about to betraie and make awaie his countrey to forainers, etc. Neuertheles forasmuche as all thinges in euery christen common wealthe ought to be done decently and according to ordre and charitie: I thinke it can not be maintened by Goddes worde, that any priuate man maie kill, except (wher execucion of iuste punishement vpon tirannes, idolaters, and traiterous gouernours is either by the hole state vtterly neglected, or the prince with the nobilitie and counsail conspire the subuersion or alteracion of their contrey and people) any priuate man haue som special inwarde commandement or surely proued mocion of God: as Moses had to kill the Egipcian, Phinees the Lecherours, and Ahud king Eglon, with suche like: or be otherwise commaunded or permitted by common autorities vpon iuste occasion and common necessitie to kill.

### III. Christopher Goodman: *How Superior Powers Oght to be Obeyd*, 1558

Alas saye you, what is this we heare? Be not the people, of themselues as sheepe without a pastor? If the Magistrates and other officers contemne their duetie in defending Gods glorie and the Lawes committed to their charge, lieth it in our power to remedie it? Shall we that are subiectes take the sworde in our handes? It is in dede as you say, a great discouraging to the people when they are not stirred vp to godlynesse by the good example of all sortes of Superiors, Magistrates and offi-cers in the faithefull executing of their office: and so muche more when they are not defended by them in their right and title, as wel concerning religion, as the free-dome of their naturall countrie: but moste of all when they, which shuld be their guydes and Capitayns, are become instrumentes to inforce them to wicked impietie. Neuertheles, all this can be no excuse for you, seing, that euil doinges of others, whether they be Lordes, Dukes, Barons, knights or any inferior officers, may not excuse you in euil. And thoghe you had no man of power vpon your parte: yet, it is a sufficient assurance for you, to haue the warrant of Godds worde vpon your side, and God him self to be your Capitayne who willeth not onely the Magistrates and officers to roote out euil from amongst them, beit, idolatrie, blasphemie or open iniurie, but the whole multitude are therwith charged also, to whom a portion of the sworde of iustice is committed, to execute the iudgementes which the Magistrates lawfully commande. And therfore if the Magistrates would whollye despice and betraye the iustice and Lawes of God, you which are subiectes with them shall be condemned except you mayntayne and defend the same Lawes agaynst them, and all others to the vttermoste of your power, that is, with all your strength, with all your harte and with all your soule, for this hath God required of you, and this haue you promised vnto him not vnder condition (if the Rulers will) but without all exceptions to do whatso euer your Lorde and God shall commande you.

### IV. The Interview of John Knox with Mary Queen of Scots, 1561

*The Queen accused John Knox that he had raised a part of her subjects against her mother and against herself; that he had written a book against her just authority, —she meant the* First Blast Against the Monstrous Regiment of Women. [*Knox answered.*]

'And, touching that Book which seemeth so highly to offend Your Majesty, it is most certain that I wrote it.'

*Queen Mary.* 'Ye think then that I have no just authority?'

*John Knox.* 'If the Realm finds no inconvenience from the government of a woman, that which they approve shall I not further disallow than within my own breast, but shall be as well content to iive under Your Grace as Paul was to live under Nero. My hope is, that so long as ye defile not your hands with the blood of the Saints of God, neither I nor that book shall either hurt you or your authority. In very deed, Madam, that book was written most especially against that wicked Jezebel of England' [*Queen Mary Tudor*].

*Queen Mary.* 'But yet ye have taught the people to receive another religion than their Princes can allow. How can that doctrine be of God, seeing that God commandeth subjects to obey their Princes?'

*John Knox.* 'Madam, as right religion took neither original strength nor authority from worldly princes, but from the Eternal God alone, so are not subjects bound to frame their religion according to the appetites of their princes.'

*Queen Mary.* 'Yea, but none of these men raised the sword against their princes.'

*John Knox.* 'God, Madam, had not given them the power and the means.'

*Queen Mary.* 'Think ye that subjects, having the power, may resist their princes?'

*John Knox.* 'If their princes exceed their bounds, Madam, no doubt they may be resisted, even by power.'

*Queen Mary.* 'Well then, I perceive that my subjects shall obey you, and not me. They shall do what they list, and not what I command; and so must I be subject to them, and not they to me.'

*John Knox.* 'God forbid that ever I take upon me to command any to obey me, or yet to set subjects at liberty to do what pleaseth them! God craves of Kings that they be foster-fathers to His Church, and commands Queens to be nurses to His people.'

*Queen Mary.* 'Yea, but ye are not the Kirk that I will nourish. I will defend the Kirk of Rome, for it is, I think, the true Kirk of God.'

*John Knox.* 'Your *will*, Madam, is no reason; neither doth your *thought* make that Roman harlot to be the true and immaculate spouse of Jesus Christ.'

*Queen Mary.* 'My conscience is not so.'

*John Knox.* 'Conscience, Madam, requireth knowledge; and I fear that right knowledge ye have none.'

*Queen Mary.* 'Ye interpret the Scriptures in one manner, and they in another. Whom shall I believe?'

*John Knox.* 'Ye shall believe God, that plainly speaketh in His Word. The Word of God is plain in itself.' [*Knox concluded.*] 'I pray God, Madam, that ye may be as blessed within the Commonwealth of Scotland, if it be the pleasure of God, as ever Deborah was in the Commonwealth of Israel.'

[*Commenting on the interview Knox said*], 'If there be not in her a proud mind, a crafty wit, and an indurate heart against God and His truth, my judgment faileth me.'

## V. *A Defence of Liberty Against Tyrants*, Preface, 1577

1) Whether subjects are bound and ought to obey princes if they command that which is against the law of God. When King Joas was crowned, we read that a

covenant was contracted between God, the king, and the people. In like manner we read that Josias and all the people entered into covenants with the Lord: we may gather from these testimonies, that in passing these covenants the high priest did covenant in the name of God in express terms, that the king and the people should take order that God might be served purely. . . . It appears, then, that the kings swear as vassals to observe the law of God, whom they confess to be Sovereign Lord over all.

Now, according to that which we have already touched, if they violate their oath, and transgress the law, we say that they have lost their kingdom. . . . If God commands one thing, and the king commands the contrary, what is that proud man that would term him a rebel who refuses to obey the king, when else he must disobey God?

Briefly, if God calls us on the one side to enrol us in His service, and the king on the other, is any man so void of reason that he will not say we must leave the king, and apply ourselves to God's service?

2) Whether it be lawful to resist a prince who doth infringe the law of God, or ruin His Church: by whom, how, and how far it is lawful. We have formerly said at the inaugurating of kings, there was a double covenant treated of, to wit "between God and the king"; and "between God and the people." . . . But who may punish the king (for here is question of corporal and temporal punishment) if it be not the whole body of the people to whom the king swears and obliges himself, no more nor less, than the people do to the king? . . . But I see well, here will be an objection made. What will you say? That a whole people, that beast of many heads, must run in a mutinous disorder, to order the business of the commonwealth?

When we speak of all the people, we understand by that, only those who hold their authority from the people, to wit, the magistrates, who are inferior to the king. . . . If the king should pass yet further, and send his lieutenants to compel us to become idolaters, and if he commands us to drive God and His service from amongst us; shall we not rather shut our gates against the king and his officers, than drive out of our town the

Lord who is the King of Kings? Let the burgesses and the citizens of towns, let the magistrates and governors of the people of God dwelling in towns, consider with themselves that they have contracted two covenants, and taken two oaths.

3) Whether private men may resist by arms. Private persons are not bound to take up arms against the prince who would compel them to become idolaters. Neither does their duty anything oblige them to it; for every one is bound to serve God in that proper vocation to which he is called.

4) Whether it be lawful to take arms for religion. In the fourth chapter of the Book of Nehemiah, we read, that one part of the people carried mortar, and another part stood ready with their weapons.

Now, if to bear arms and to make war be a thing lawful, can there possibly be found any war more just than that which is taken in hand by the command of the superior, for the defence of the church, and the preservation of the faithful? . . . Although then the church be not increased by arms, notwithstanding it may be justly preserved by the means of arms. I say further, that those that die in so holy a war are no less the martyrs of Jesus Christ than their brethren who were put to death for religion.

# — Reading No. 12 —

# PERSECUTION AND LIBERTY[12]

*Catholics and Protestants alike engaged in persecution in the sixteenth century. Catholics persecuted Protestants, Protestants persecuted those who were more Protestant. The presuppositions were similar, that heresy is an affront to the majesty of the Supreme Governor of the Universe, worse than a similar offense against an earthly monarch, therefore doubly subject to the penalties for lèse majesté, and treason. Heresy counterfeits truth, kills not bodies but souls, and brings calamities upon the commonwealth. Consequently the penalties for counterfeiting, murder, even parricide and conspiracy against the commonwealth, all apply. One notes that the Catholic King Francis I is especially mindful of the public calamities attributed to rising Protestantism.*

*Protestant persecution was fierce against the Anabaptists. A man, who held both Anabaptist and Antitrinitarian views, was Michael Servetus, who was burned in effigy by the Catholics in France, in actuality by the*

[12] The documents in this reading are taken from: (I) *Cronique du Roy Françoys Premier*, ed. Georges Guiffrey (Paris, 1860), pp. 113-29, greatly condensed; (II) Translated by R. H. Bainton in *Hunted Heretic* (Boston, 1953), pp. 207-209; (III) Passages culled from the historical chronicle of the Hutterian Brethren by Harold Bender and published in "The Anabaptist Vision," *Church History*, XIII, 1 (March, 1944), p. 7; (IV) *De Haereticis coercendis* and *Traité des Hérétiques*, both 1553. The French was reprinted by Eugene Choisy (Geneva, 1913), the Latin appeared in facsimile edited by Sepe Van der Woude (Geneva, 1954). R. H. Bainton brought out an English translation with critical introduction and notes in *Records of Civilization*, XXII (Columbia University, New York, 1935). The opening and closing portions of the dedication are here given from pages 121-23 and 134-35.

*Protestants at Geneva. The sentence refers to his previous career. He had published two books* On the Errors of the Trinity *(1531) and the* Restitution of Christianity *(1553). For a biography see R. H. Bainton,* Hunted Heretic *(Beacon Press, Boston, 1953). Observe that, although John Calvin denounced Servetus, he was tried and condemned by a lay tribunal. Sebastian Castellio, who issued the anonymous pamphlet* Concerning Heretics *(1554), had been a teacher at Geneva and was at the time teaching at Basel. Many of his ideas were Erasmian, that deeds are more important in God's eyes than creeds, that sincerity is to be preferred to correctness, that the beliefs punished by fire are uncertain. This is apparent because they are controverted. Still worse they are unimportant, for the significant truths are those as to which there is agreement.*

✓           ✓           ✓

I. Catholic Persecution of Protestants: The Procession in Paris, January 29, 1535, under Francis I

The most Christian king [*Francis I*], our sovereign lord, knowing that certain damnable heresies and blasphemies swarmed in his kingdom and desiring with the aid of God to extirpate the same decreed that a sacred procession should be held in this city of Paris on the twenty-first day [*actually the twenty-ninth*] of January 1535. The streets were adorned with gorgeous tapestries and the crowds held in order by archers in uniform. First came the crosses and banners of the Diocese of Paris followed by citizens and merchants carrying torches, then the four monastic orders with relics, next priests and canons of the parochial churches with relics, and the monks of Saint Martin with the head of that saint. Another carried the head of Saint Philip, one of the most precious relics in Paris. The body of Madame Saincte Geneviève was borne by six citizens in their shirts. Then followed the Canons of Notre Dame, the Rector of the University, and the Swiss Guard with their band of violins, trumpets, and cornets. Among the relics were the true cross of Christ and the crown of thorns and the lance that pierced his side. Then came a great number of the archbishops and bishops with the blood

of our Saviour, the rod of Moses, and the head of John
the Baptist. Next the cardinals. The precious body of our
Lord was carried by archdeacons on a velvet cushion of
violet adorned with *fleurs de lys.* Following the Holy
Sacrament came the King alone with bare head carrying a lighted taper. After him marched Monseigneur the
Cardinal of Lorraine, then all the princes and knights
and members of the *Parlement,* etc. The Holy Sacrament was taken to the church of Notre Dame and there
deposited with great reverence by the Bishop of Paris.
Then the King and his children, the Queen and her
attendants and many notables had dinner with the Bishop
of Paris. After dinner the King made a speech against
the execrable and damnable opinions dispersed throughout his kingdom. While the King, the Queen, and their
court were with the Bishop of Paris, into their presence
were brought six of the said heretics and in front of the
church of Notre Dame they were burned alive. A number of other heretics went to the stake during the days
following so that all over Paris one saw gibbets by which
the people were filled with terror.

II. Protestant Persecution of a Heretic: The Sentence
Pronounced on Michael Servetus, October 27, 1553

The sentence pronounced against Michel Servet de
Villeneufve of the Kingdom of Aragon in Spain who
some twenty-three or twenty-four years ago printed a
book at Hagenau in Germany against the Holy Trinity
containing many great blasphemies to the scandal of the
said churches of Germany, the which book he freely
confesses to have printed in the teeth of the remonstrances made to him by the learned and evangelical
doctors of Germany. In consequence he became a fugi-
tive from Germany. Nevertheless, he continued in his
errors and, in order the more to spread the venom of his
heresy, he printed secretly a book in Vienne of Dauphiny
full of the said heresies and horrible, execrable blasphemies against the Holy Trinity, against the Son of
God, against the baptism of infants and the foundations
of the Christian religion. He confesses that in this book
he called believers in the Trinity Trinitarians and atheists.
He calls this Trinity a diabolical monster with three
heads. He blasphemes detestably against the Son of God,

saying that Jesus Christ is not the Son of God from eternity. He calls infant baptism an invention of the devil and sorcery. His execrable blasphemies are scandalous against the majesty of God, the Son of God and the Holy Spirit. This entails the murder and ruin of many souls. Moreover he wrote a letter to one of our ministers in which, along with other numerous blasphemies, he declared our holy evangelical religion to be without faith and without God and that in place of God we have a three-headed Cerberus. He confesses that because of this abominable book he was made a prisoner at Vienne and perfidiously escaped. He has been burned there in effigy together with five bales of his books. Nevertheless, having been in prison in our city, he persists maliciously in his detestable errors and calumniates true Christians and faithful followers of the immaculate Christian tradition.

Wherefore we Syndics, judges of criminal cases in this city, having witnessed the trial conducted before us at the instance of our Lieutenant against you "Michel Servet de Villeneufve" of the Kingdom of Aragon in Spain, and having seen your voluntary and repeated confessions and your books, judge that you, Servetus, have for a long time promulgated false and thoroughly heretical doctrine, despising all remonstrances and corrections and that you have with malicious and perverse obstinacy sown and divulged even in printed books opinions against God the Father, the Son and the Holy Spirit, in a word against the fundamentals of the Christian religion, and that you have tried to make a schism and trouble the Church of God by which many souls may have been ruined and lost, a thing horrible, shocking, scandalous and infectious. And you have had neither shame nor horror of setting yourself against the divine Majesty and the Holy Trinity, and so you have obstinately tried to infect the world with your stinking heretical poison. . . . For these and others reasons, desiring to purge the Church of God of such infection and cut off the rotten member, having taken counsel with our citizens and having invoked the name of God to give just judgment . . . having God and the Holy Scriptures before our eyes, speaking in the name of the Father, Son and Holy Spirit, we now in writing give final sentence and condemn you, Michael Servetus, to be bound and taken to Champel and there attached to a stake and burned with your book to ashes. And so you shall finish your days and give an example to others who would commit the like.

### III. Anabaptist Martyrs

They had drunk of the waters which had flowed from God's sanctuary, yea, the water of life. They realized that God helped them to bear the cross and to overcome the bitterness of death. The fire of God burned within them. Their tent they had pitched not here upon earth, but in eternity, and of their faith they had a foundation and assurance. Their faith blossomed as a lily, their loyalty as a rose, their piety and sincerity as the flower of the garden of God. The angel of the Lord battled for them that they could not be deprived of the helmet of salvation. Therefore they bore all torture and agony without fear. The things of this world they counted in their holy mind only as shadows, having the assurance of greater things. They were so drawn unto God that they knew nothing, sought nothing, desired nothing, loved nothing but God alone. Therefore they had more patience in their suffering than their enemies in tormenting them.

. . . The persecutors thought they could dampen and extinguish the fire of God. But the prisoners sang in their prisons and rejoiced so that the enemies outside became much more fearful than the prisoners and did not know what to do with them. . . .

From the shedding of such innocent blood arose Christians everywhere, for all this persecution did not take place without fruit. . . .

### IV. Plea for Religious Liberty: Sebastian Castellio, *On the Coercion of Heretics,* 1554

Most Illustrious Prince [*Duke Christoph of Württemberg*], suppose you had told your subjects that you would come to them at some uncertain time and had commanded them to make ready to go forth clad in white garments to meet you whenever you might appear. What would you do if, on your return, you discovered that they had taken no thought for the white robes but instead were disputing among themselves concerning your person? Some were saying that you were in France, others that you were in Spain; some that you would come on a horse, others in a chariot; some were asserting that you would appear with a great equipage, others that you would be unattended. Would this please you?

Suppose further that the controversy was being conducted not merely by words but by blows and swords, and that one group wounded and killed the others who did not agree with them. "He will come on a horse," one would say.

"No, in a chariot," another would retort.

"You lie."

"You're the liar. Take that." He punches him.

"And take that in the belly." The other stabs.

Would you, O Prince, commend such citizens? Suppose, however, that some did their duty and followed your command to prepare the white robes, but the others oppressed them on that account and put them to death. Would you not rigorously destroy such scoundrels?

But what if these homicides claimed to have done all this in your name and in accord with your command, even though you had previously expressly forbidden it? Would you not consider that such outrageous conduct deserved to be punished without mercy? Now I beg you, most Illustrious Prince, to be kind enough to hear why I say these things.

Christ is the Prince of this world who on His departure from the earth foretold to men that He would return some day at an uncertain hour, and He commanded them to prepare white robes for His coming, that is to say, that they should live together in a Christian manner, amicably, without controversy and contention, loving one another. But consider now, I beg you, how well we discharge our duty.

How many are there who show the slightest concern to prepare the white robe? Who is there who bends every effort to live in this world in a saintly, just, and religious manner in the expectation of the coming of the Lord? For nothing is there so little concern. The true fear of God and charity are fallen and grown cold. Our life is spent in contention and in every manner of sin. We dispute, not as to the way by which we may come to

Christ, which is to correct our lives, but rather as to the
state and office of Christ, where He now is and what He
is doing, how He is seated at the right hand of the
Father, and how He is one with the Father; likewise
with regard to the Trinity, predestination, free will; so,
also, of God, the angels, the state of souls after this life
and other like things, which do not need to be known
for salvation by faith (for the publicans and sinners were
saved without this knowledge), nor indeed can they be
known before the heart is pure (for to see these things
is to see God Himself, who cannot be seen save by the
pure in heart, as the text says, "Blessed are the pure in
heart for they shall see God)." Nor if these are known
do they make a man better, as Paul says, "Though I
understand all mysteries and have not love it profiteth me
nothing." This perverse curiosity engenders worse evils.
Men are puffed up with knowledge or with a false
opinion of knowledge and look down upon others. Pride
is followed by cruelty and persecution so that now
scarcely anyone is able to endure another who differs at
all from him. Although opinions are almost as numerous
as men, nevertheless there is hardly any sect which does
not condemn all others and desire to reign alone. Hence
arise banishments, chains, imprisonments, stakes, and
gallows and this miserable rage to visit daily penalties
upon those who differ from the mighty about matters
hitherto unknown, for so many centuries disputed, and
not yet cleared up.

If, however, there is someone who strives to prepare
the white robe, that is, to live justly and innocently, then
all others with one accord cry out against him if he differ
from them in anything, and they confidently pronounce
him a heretic on the ground that he seeks to be justified
by works. Horrible crimes of which he never dreamed
are attributed to him and the common people are preju-
diced by slander until they consider it a crime merely to
hear him speak. Hence arises such cruel rage that some
are so incensed by calumny as to be infuriated when the
victim is first strangled instead of being burned alive at
a slow fire. . . .

O Creator and King of the world, dost Thou see these
things? Art Thou become so changed, so cruel, so contrary to Thyself? When Thou wast on earth none was

more mild, more clement, more patient of injury. As a sheep before the shearer Thou wast dumb. When scourged spat upon, mocked, crowned with thorns, and crucified shamefully among thieves, Thou didst pray for them who did Thee this wrong. Art Thou now so changed? I beg Thee in the name of Thy Father, dost Thou now command that those who do not understand Thy precepts as the mighty demand, be drowned in water, cut with lashes to the entrails, sprinkled with salt, dismembered by the sword, burned at a slow fire, and otherwise tortured in every manner and as long as possible? Dost Thou, O Christ, command and approve of these things? Are they Thy vicars who make these sacrifices? Art Thou present when they summon Thee and dost Thou eat human flesh? If Thou, Christ, dost these things or if Thou commandest that they be done, what hast Thou left for the devil? Dost Thou the very same things as Satan? O blasphemies and shameful audacity of men, who dare to attribute to Christ that which they do by the command and at the instigation of Satan!

# BIBLIOGRAPHY

I. GENERAL SURVEYS:
  Grimm, Harold, *The Era of the Reformation* (New York, 1954).
  Lindsay, Thomas M., *A History of the Reformation*, 2 vols. (1916-1917).
  Smith, Preserved, *The Age of the Reformation* (1920).
  Bainton, Roland H., *The Reformation of the Sixteenth Century* (1952, paperback 1956).
II. LUTHER:
  Bainton, R. H., *Here I Stand: A Life of Martin Luther* (1950).
  Boehmer, H., *Road to Reformation* (1946).

Mackinnon, James, *Luther and the Reformation.*
4 vols. (1925-30).

McGiffert, A. C., *Martin Luther* (1917).

Rupp, E. G., *Luther's Progress to the Diet of Worms* (1951).

Schwiebert, Ernst, *Luther and His Times; The Reformation from a New Perspective* (St. Louis, 1950).

Smith, Preserved, *Life and Letters of Martin Luther* (1911).

Watson, Philip S., *Let God Be God* (1947).

III. ZWINGLI:

Farner, Oskar, *Zwingli the Reformer: His Life and Work* (New York, 1952).

IV. CALVIN:

Hunt, R. N. C., *Calvin* (1933).

Reyburn, H. Y., *John Calvin* (1914).

Walker, W., *John Calvin* (1906).

V. THE ANABAPTISTS:

Bender, Harold, *The Life and Letters of Conrad Grebel* (1950-      ).

Horsch, J., *Menno Simons* (1916).

Littell, Franklin, *The Anabaptist View of the Church* (1952).

VI. FRANCE:

Kelly, C. G., *French Protestantism 1559-62* (1918).

Palm, F. C., *Calvinism and the Religious Wars* (1932).

Palm, F. C., *Politics and Religion in Sixteenth Century France* (1927).

Thompson, J. W., *The Wars of Religion in France* (1909).

Zopf, Otto, *The Huguenots* (1942).

VII. ITALY:

Brown, G. K., *Italy and the Reformation to 1550* (1933).

Church, Frederic C., *The Italian Reformers 1534-64* (1932).

VIII. SPAIN:

Wilkens, C. A., *Spanish Protestants in the Sixteenth Century* (1897).

IX. NETHERLANDS:
Harrison, F., *William the Silent* (1897).

X. SCANDINAVIA:
Bergendorf, Conrad, *Olavus Petri . . . : A Study of the Swedish Reformation* (1928).

XI. POLAND:
Fox, P., *The Reformation in Poland* (1924).

XII. ENGLAND AND SCOTLAND:
Constant, G., *The Reformation in England,* 2 vols. (1934-42).

Parker, T. M., *The English Reformation to 1558* (1950).

Percy, E., *John Knox* (1905).

Rupp, E. G., *Studies in the Making of the English Protestant Tradition* (1947).

XIII. THE STRUGGLE FOR RECOGNITION AND LIBERTY:
Bainton, R. H., *The Travail of Religious Liberty* (1951).

XIV. SOCIAL EFFECTS AND INTERPRETATION:
Allen, J. W., *A History of Political Thought in the Sixteenth Century* (1928).

McGiffert, A. C., *Protestant Thought Before Kant* (1911).

Pauck, Wilhelm, *The Heritage of the Reformation* (1950).

Tawney, R. H., *Religion and the Rise of Capitalism* (1926).

Weber, Max, *The Protestant Ethic and the Spirit of Capitalism* (1930).

# INDEX